aracteristics of the
Mastiff

erican Kennel Club breed standard)

Topline: In profile the topline should be straight, level, and firm.

Back: Muscular, powerful, and straight.

Loins: Wide and muscular.

Tail: Set on moderately high and reaching to the hocks or a little below. Wide at the root, tapering to the end.

Size: Dogs, minimum, 30 inches at the shoulder. Bitches, minimum, 27 inches at the shoulder.

Substance: Massive, heavy boned, with a powerful muscle structure.

Proportion: Rectangular, the length of the dog from forechest to rump is somewhat longer than the height at the withers.

Underline: There should be a reasonable, but not exaggerated, tuck-up.

Coat: Outer coat straight, coarse, and of moderately short length. Undercoat dense, short, and close lying.

Color: Fawn, apricot, or brindle. Brindle should have fawn or apricot as a background color which should be completely covered with very dark stripes.

Hindquarters: Broad, wide and muscular. Second thighs well developed, leading to a strong hock joint. Stifle joint is moderately angulated matching the front. Rear legs are wide apart and parallel when viewed from the rear.

Mastiff
◇
By Christina de Lima-Netto

Contents

AUTHOR'S DEDICATION
*To my husband,
Chema Sanmillan,
with all my love.*

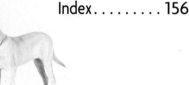

KENNEL CLUB BOOKS® MASTIFF
ISBN: 1-59378-337-X

Copyright © 2003, 2007 • Kennel Club Books® • A Division of BowTie, Inc.
40 Broad Street, Freehold, NJ 07728 USA
Cover Design Patented: US 6,435,559 B2 • Printed in South Korea

Photography by Carol Ann Johnson with additional photographs by:

Norvia Behling, T.J. Calhoun, Carolina Biological Supply, Ana Maria Bodim, Michelle Carstens, Anne Marie Class, Doskocil, Lisa Edwards-Filu, Isabelle Francais, James Hayden-Yoav, James R. Hayden, RBP, Magaret Hope, Bill Jonas, Dwight R. Kuhn, Dr. Dennis Kunkel, Christina de Lima-Netto, Antonio Phillippe, Mikki Pet Products, Phototake, Jean Claude Revy, Dr. Andrew Spielman, Alice van Kempen and Charlene Via.

Illustrations by Patricia Peters.

The publisher would like to thank all of the owners of the Mastiffs featured in this book, including Mary Ann Alternative, Cathy Babins, Gregory Beasley, Lisa Edwards-Filu, Sherry L. Eisenhuth, Andy Filu, Connie Gard, Mr. T. and Mrs. S. Green, Robert S. Jones, Christina de Lima-Netto, Kennel de Quelque Part, Mr. J. and Mrs. C. Rischmiller, George Williams and Keith and Margaret Yates.

Deriving from the ancient dogs of the Old World, the Mastiff is one of the oldest breeds of dog. Today's breed is massive, powerful and impressive in every imaginable way.

HISTORY OF THE

MASTIFF

ORIGIN OF THE DOG

As we gaze at our giant Mastiffs, snoozing by our feet or sleeping comfortably on our sofas, every proud owner likes to believe that his dog is the direct descendant of a brave and noble molosser from centuries past. Such a romantic notion makes us feel that our Mastiff is more dignified and pure! While owners of most pure-bred dogs would like to have this sense of satisfaction, most cannot. Yet, the Mastiff indeed derives from ancient dogs from the Old World, and there is plenty of evidence to substantiate this claim.

How the domestic dog actually came into existence is still quite a mystery. We cannot be certain whether early humans first approached wolves or wolves first approached humans. Nevertheless, the absolute truth is that such association has been beneficial for both species and has allowed canines to become members of the human family.

For years, archaeologists ignored canine skeletal remains found at the sites of early human settlements. This has prevented scientists from determining the original connection between humans and canines. Yet, we have evidence of their mythical relationship from depictions in ancient pottery, sculpture and carvings. Thus, the first reference to the dog-and-man relationship derives from a later period. Findings indicate that in 10,000 BC, the Earth's canine population was not greater than 10,000,000. These canines were scattered throughout the continents and were all used for the purpose of hunting. By the 16th century,

Who dares awaken the noble giant? Who would doubt this molosser's purity and bravery?

A Mastiff shown in a bas-relief dated about 2200 BC. It is on display at the British Museum in London.

later, when humans settled down to a more stationary existence, their dogs did the same. At this time, our ancestors must have noticed that their canine allies could also be used for other purposes, such as guarding and shepherding.

Thus, dogs progressively began to acquire a different status in the developing human society. Some human communities erected altars and worshipped dogs as minor gods. The Egyptians, for example, adored Seth, the god of evil, and Anubis, the god of death; both gods were represented by half-human and half-dog or jackal forms. Others considered dogs as magical or mythical entities. For example, dying Aryans were left in the company of their dogs since they believed that dogs could offer them spiritual support and help them find the way to reach the other side. Yet, there were others that considered dogs as demonical, fearful, filthy beings.

canine population was estimated to be about 350 million world-wide, and, at the end of the 20th century, there were as many as three billion dogs around the world. Today only a small percentage is still used for hunting tasks, but dogs are used to perform many other important duties.

The explanation is very simple. If early domesticated dogs were used mainly for hunting by nomadic peoples, then

Mastiffs hunting the wild horse as depicted in this Assyrian bas-relief dated about 650 BC.

How and when the kind of selection that made it possible to differentiate and develop phenotypes and genotypes among the canine species began is not yet clear. It is one of those mysteries that perhaps one day archaeology will answer.

ANCIENT DOGS

While much of ancient dog history is based largely on conjecture, we do know for certain that various ancient peoples, such as the Assyrians, Babylonians, Chinese, Egyptians, Medes, Mesopotamians and Persians, used dogs for different purposes according to the dogs' sizes. Such purposes were based on a deliberate selection, more or less artificial, which paved the way toward the highly defined dog breeds we have today.

Those dogs with more ferocious temperaments were used in battles and to guard temples and palaces. Other fierce dogs were used for hunting large animals and, later, in baiting exhibitions, where they were pitted against all sorts of wild beasts and, later still, against other aggressive dogs. Dogs were also used as executioners, where the dog would be expected to consume a condemned prisoner alive!

Other individuals were used to watch over the herds; therefore, they were raised among cows, sheep and goats from puppyhood.

GENUS *CANIS*
Dogs and wolves are members of the genus *Canis*. Wolves are known scientifically as *Canis lupus* while dogs are known as *Canis domesticus*. Dogs and wolves are known to interbreed. The term "canine" derives from the Latin-derived word *Canis*. The term "dog" has no scientific basis but has been used for thousands of years. The origin of the word "dog" has never been authoritatively ascertained.

Recent DNA studies have proved that the taming of wolves is traced back to 100,000 years ago. This means that dogs have been accompanying our ancestors for longer than we had thought.

The purpose of this was to acclimate the dogs with their charges, the herds. In this way, the dogs would protect their herds from the attacks of wolves and other wild animals in the same way that they would protect their own families. Finally, there were dogs that lived under their masters' roofs to protect their properties and families or simply to serve as companions.

Dogs were utilized not only in Asia but also in Europe, where the Romans and Greeks on one side

Depicting the Assyrians leading Assurbanipal's Mastiff to a hunt, this bas-relief from the Palace of Nineveh is dated about 650 BC. It is on display at the British Museum.

and the Celts, Iberians, Germans, Normans and Saxons on the other used dogs for hunting, guarding, warring and shepherding. Humans around the Old World were discovering that dogs could play significant roles in their developing societies.

TRADE AND EXCHANGE

The ancient world was active in trade and other cultural relations. Usually these exchanges were conducted under peaceful, amicable conditions, but, at other times, these "acquisitions" were the results of bloody wars and territorial occupation. In cases where a community was conquered or colonized, the dogs that lived among that community were taken and exported, like everything else of value in the fallen culture. Thus, dogs from any people conquered by the

A prolific sire of his day, Eng. Ch. Crown Prince was born in February 1880 and was exhibited by Dr. L.S. Forbes-Winslow of London and bred by Mr. H.G. Woolmore.

Romans, for instance, could have been interbred with dogs on Continental Europe and beyond.

Sometimes the dogs were so highly prized that they were used as currency. Despite our lack of specific historical references, this theory explains how dogs with similar characteristics and uses inhabited different parts of the civilized world while being named differently by the communities who owned them.

This theory also leads us to accept the fact that we cannot know for certain whether our Mastiff came before or after the mastiff types that existed in other lands. Like the scrambled riddle about the chicken and the egg, we may never know the true origins of the Mastiff. Unfortunately, as it has happened with the origins of most other breeds,

BRAINS AND BRAWN

Since dogs have been inbred for centuries, their physical and mental characteristics are constantly being changed to suit man's desires for hunting, retrieving, scenting, guarding and warming their masters' laps. During the past 150 years, dogs have been judged according to physical characteristics as well as functional abilities. Few breeds can boast a genuine balance between physique, working ability and temperament.

An old German, woodcut estimated around 1534 AD, showing what might possibly be Mastiff crosses.

the Mastiff's are shrouded in the mystery of time. Let us investigate how the ancestors of the Mastiff appeared in ancient times.

GIANTS FROM THE PAST
There is no doubt that those dogs that gave way to the Mastiff of today were very large animals, used at different times for warring, shepherding and guarding, as well as for transporting and pulling heavy loads and for fighting against other beasts. These ancient dogs were brave, ferocious animals, physically strong and capable of enduring great pain. Only a survivor like the Mastiff could have endured the test of time.

The Mastiff's ancestors could have had either long, thick, woolly coats or short, close-lying coats. Some dogs were solid-colored while others were bi-colored or tri-colored in black and white, chestnut, red, blue, black or brindle. The muzzles varied greatly: some dogs had short, flat muzzles; others had square, wide muzzles and others had rather elongated, narrow muzzles. The ears of some dogs were set high, forming a "V" shape. Body type varied considerably as well. Their bodies could have been somewhat

MOLOSSIA, GREECE
Molossia was a settlement from Mycenæ, located in Greece's continental area, between the limits of Mount Pindus and the origins of the Thiamis River. Later on, during the spread of the Greek civilization, it became a city-state. Its inhabitants were cavemen. They were mainly shepherds and their dogs were used for the driving and guarding of herds. The weather was cold and rainy in an area surrounded by mountains.

compact, wide and square, or narrow and long. Every physical feature of these ancient dogs depended upon how the humans bred them, how they were kept, the climates in which they lived and, of course, the duties for which they were employed.

Countless narrations, accounts and legends from early civilizations around the world have been told and retold over the years. Popular narrators may have adorned or exaggerated these stories with their imaginative twists, while the more accredited historians have pared these accounts down to the most authentic information. The stories abound about these large brave dogs, standing by man's side through devastating times and saving humans from mortal danger. Some dogs won favor with kings and noblemen, as well as the affection of entire cities. Today, these great dogs remain a part of the traditions and legends of many nations, filtering their way into our current recounting of the history of the Mastiff.

It would be impossible to give way, in this book, to the very many accounts and legends that have survived, but at least a few should be mentioned in order to help us better understand the unique character traits of this colossal canine breed that we have named the Mastiff.

LEGENDARY DOGS
According to legend, some "fifty large-sized, fierce-looking dogs of the mastiff-type protected, even at the expense of their own lives, the city of Corinthia (ancient Greece), which had been

Owner Mark Beaufoy with his Eng. Ch. Nero, who was bred by Rev. J. Bulkley Jones in 1875. Nero became one of the most popular champions of the breed in that era.

invaded by the Barbarians. This happened while the city's inhabitants were deep asleep. Forty-nine of these dogs died in the battle. The sole survivor was rewarded with a silver collar. Later on, the Corinthians erected a monument to pay tribute to those brave four-legged warriors that defended their city-state from invaders."

A Celtic legend tells of "one of the most important warriors named Cu Chulainn, who took his name from 'Culann's dog,' owned by a free, rich, well-respected man with the same name. This man was at the service of King Conchobar. The king visited him, accompanied by his servants and his nephew, who was the warrior Cu Chulainn. As Culann felt incapable of attending his royal guests at the same time that he watched over the village, he entitled his dog to surveillance. Culann released his dog after making sure that all inhabitants were inside the village and that all guests were safe, just in case the dog took any of the visitors for an intruder and mistakenly attacked him while performing his duty.

"But both Culann and King Conchobar forgot that the king's nephew was still outside. It was only after they heard the screaming, growling and barking coming from outside that they noticed what had happened and realized

that the life of the king's nephew was at stake. To their astonishment, they found that the fates had twisted in the boy's favor—the king's nephew had killed Culann's dog! Culann, then, bitterly complained to the king for the loss of such a loyal and valuable dog, the one and only capable of defending the whole village from the attack of thieves and wolves. In remorse, the boy decided to become the village's new guardian."

What is most interesting is that the bard who recorded this account also details how the dog guarded the village. He wrote, "The dog climbed a hill and watched over the settlement from there, lying down, his head resting on his fore legs," a description very similar to the way our modern Mastiffs guard our homes today.

Even though these two legends may have been spiced up by the narrators, for sake of more romantic stories, there are many other historical references to these large dogs, which resemble our modern Mastiffs in many ways. Following are some noteworthy examples that help us piece together the puzzle of the Mastiff's origins.

HISTORICAL REFERENCES
One of the earliest references comes from the Roman poet Virgil (70–19 BC) who, around 39 BC,

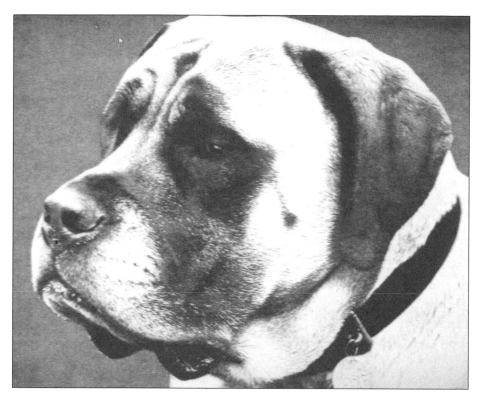

A historical Mastiff born in 1929, this is Eng. Ch. Volo of Ileden.

dedicated some verses to dogs in his pastoral poetry entitled "Bucolic." Virgil referred to the Roman tradition of cropping dogs' ears, explaining that the practice was not performed for esthetic reasons, but to prevent wolves and foxes from biting these vulnerable part of the dog's body. In a later poem, entitled "Georgic," Virgil also suggests that it would be interesting to feed Spartan hunting dogs and the "brave molossian dogs" with fat serum.

Historian and geographer Strabo (64 BC–20 AD) said, "Britain produces corn, cattle, gold, silver and iron, together with skins, slaves and dogs of a superior breed for the chase. The Gauls use these dogs in war, as well as others of their own breed."

We cannot overlook Grattius (circa 19–8 BC), who wrote in *Cynegetican* about the Parthian, Celtic, Gelonian, Median, Arcadian, Thessalian, Hyrcanian and Acarnian dogs, among others. When referring to the Romans' conquest of Britain, Grattius specifically cites that "the 'pugnaces' of Epirus were taken to

fight against the 'pugnaces' of Britain and the latter ended up killing the former."

Another quotation, from the Carthaginian poet Nemesianus, in his work *Cynegetica*, written around 283–284 AD, praised the celerity and courage of "the great British dogs." It also goes into detail about dogs such as the Spartan, Pannonian, Umbrian, Libyan, Hispanic and Molossian.

References to Molossian dogs appear many times in ancient writings. Even the great Aristotle mentioned them: "The dogs from Molossia are no different whatsoever from others (...) although the most famous for their courage and the way they do their work are those resulting from the crossing of dogs from Molossia and Laconia." Aristotle added that "the largest ones, however, are the ones from Epiroto" and he described them as "large-sized, strong dogs, of heavy muzzle..." He added later that "their size, aspect and temperament are such that some believe them to be descendants of Cerberus, the very dog Hercules brought from Hell." All of those dogs were named for their places of origin, which was a common practice in ancient times. Nevertheless, they did not necessarily constitute well-defined types or breeds.

According to Studer and Strebel in 1905, "Since the ancient times, men tried to define the different types of dogs.

Beginning with the ones which, by their physical strength and powerful bite, could defend men and their herds from the attack of more powerful enemies and, at the same time, hunt larger wild animals and keep domestic animals under control." Such powerful dogs are the most likely forerunners of the modern Mastiff and the other large guarding breeds we know today.

DIFFERENT NAMES

The fact is that we may never find the clues to the real origin of the modern Mastiff, but it is believed, without doubt, that their ancestors played an important role in the history of our own evolution. These dogs had close relationships with our own ancestors, whenever and wherever they were needed, and in whatever capacity, no matter the names by which they were called.

As previously stated, the vast majority of the early dog types were named after their places of origin. As dog types developed more specifically, they were named for their uses in their language of origin: "pugnax" or "pugnaces" (for those used in battles); "alanos," "alans," "allans" or "allaunts" (for those

The Spanish Mastiff is growing tremendously in popularity both inside and outside its native Spanish borders.

used in hunting); "bandogs," "band-dogges," "bandadocs," "tie-dogs" or "tydogs" (after the leather "bands" or collars on their necks); "mastives," "massivus" or "massifs" (for their large size); "mastys," "mastyfs," "mastyfes" or "mestyfs" (for their blood mix).

During the reign of England's King Henry II (1133–1189), founder of the Plantagenet dynasty, the term "mastiff" was used for the first time to define a type of corpulent dog (not yet the breed we know today) of very variable height and other physical

The Tibetan Mastiff is an Asian guard/war dog. Authorities believe that this breed is the fore-runner of all molosser-type dogs.

> **ABOUT BANDOGS**
> It is very likely that "bandogs" or "band dogges" took their names from the wide leather bands or collars around their necks that kept them tied all day long. They were only released in the evenings to perform their tasks as guardians.

traits. These dogs were considered superior for guarding and fighting other beasts, although every dog falling into this new category did not have to share each and every characteristic.

The use of the term "mastiff" spread after the Normans conquered England. It was originally spelled with only one "f," probably due to its Latin origin. Another reason could be that the Normans, who defeated the Saxons in Hastings during the 1066 Christmas celebrations and crowned William "the Conqueror," spoke French and used their own language in all government meetings as well as in the newly created nobility circles. Later on, Normans also used French to write the "Forest Laws," which were dictated by numerous English kings, descendants of Henry II.

Some English rulers such as John I and Henry III ordered the horrendous mutilation of all large dogs of the "mastiff" type that were not owned by the noble

The Neapolitan Mastiff can weigh as much as the Mastiff and also derives from ancient molosser types.

people of their kingdoms. These measures were taken to prevent the lower classes from using their dogs to hunt large animals, which was only allowed if approved by the royals.

BEAR FIGHTS

Fights held between Mastiffs and other wild beasts turned not only some nearly unbeatable bears but also some dogs into heroes. The victories of one of the bears, known as "Young black-face," became the theme for many ballads sung by the bards. The bear won more than 20 battles, but three Mastiffs finally defeated him in a rule fight, where neither the bear nor the dogs wore collars for protection.

DOG FIGHTING

At the court of England's Henry VIII (1491–1547), known for his taste for sending his wives to the scaffolds and seeing their heads cut off, a new normative was dictated. His Royal Majesty forbid dogs at court and one of his regulations said, "No dogs to be kept in court. The king's highness also directly forbids anyone, whoever they are, to presume to keep at court any greyhound, mastiff, hound or other dog, except for small spaniels for ladies and other folk, nor to bring dogs to court, except by the King or Queen's order."

Yet the King himself and his daughters, Mary Stuart and Elizabeth I, encouraged and protected dog fights and baiting contests. These exhibitions were held in places known as "gardens." The most renowned was the Paris Garden, where, according to Erasmus (from *Adagia*, 1506), many herds of bears were kept to fight dogs. Another chronicler of the time, named Lupton, said in 1632 that "more than a beautiful garden, this place was a fetid shelter where the scandalous, the bloody butchers, the astute thieves, the obscene and the drunken all had their rendezvous."

These exhibitions went on for centuries, and even though this may shock some readers, these disgusting displays allowed for some greater selectivity in breeding as fanciers strove to produce stronger, more fearless dogs. Similar qualities were selected for in dogs used for war purposes and hunting large game. When dog fights were finally outlawed by the end of the 19th century and these dogs lost their main purpose, the dogs suddenly were faced with the threat of extinction.

CONSOLIDATION OF TYPE

Some of these large dogs were then used for other purposes, such as cart-pulling and other modes of transportation, but, by

The Mastiff has been the subject of many paintings by the great masters. "The Children of Charles I with Mastiff" is the title of this Van Dyck painting on display at London's National Portrait Gallery.

and large, they were less practical than mules or donkeys. The dogs that escaped extinction were owned by the gentlemen that we will call "the first British dog breeders." Men like John Crabtree, Dr. Forbes-Winslow, Bill George, T.H.V. Lukey, Mellor, Edwin Nichols, W.K. Taunton, Commissioner Thompson and, later, his grandson J.W. Thompson, dedicated themselves to the Mastiff dogs.

The famous Lyme Hall and Bold Hall lines were directly linked through the many crosses that occurred between the two over the many years. The families behind these lines became linked after the marriage in 1612 of Sir Piers Leigh's great-granddaughter Anna to Richard Bold, a rich landowner from Lancashire. It was this Sir Piers Leigh who was the hero of the battle of Agincourt, repeatedly referenced by Shakespeare in his verse. He fought in the Hundred Years' War, accompanied by his Mastiff bitch, the same dog that, according to legend, later guarded his dead body on its return to England and during his funeral.

Eng. Ch. Wolsey was born in 1873 and was considered the best brindle Mastiff of the day.

THE FIRST BREED STANDARD

Even in the mid-19th century, when John Crabtree and Bill George and their contemporaries Lukey and Thompson assumed the selective breeding of the Mastiff, there was a great disparity of criteria. Crabtree and George were in favor of producing athletic dogs, able to move freely, even if this meant breeding some-what smaller dogs. The other two breeders preferred larger dogs, even if the dog's movement and agility were compromised for the sake of size.

Then came M.B. Wynn from The Elms, Rothley, in Leicester-shire, England. He was the founder of the UK's first Mastiff club (1874) and wrote *The History of the Mastiff* in January 1886. This was the first treatise ever written on the breed. According to Mr. Wynn himself, the book was "gathered from sculpture, pottery, carving, paintings and engravings; also from various authors, with remarks on the same." He signed his book, "M.B. Wynn, Honorary Secretary and Treasurer of the late Mastiff Club and Breeder and Exhibitor of many prize Mastiffs." This man was in favor of raising dogs with more massive, square heads and flatter muzzles. He showed his position by awarding a dog named Crown Prince several times in the first dog shows.

Mr. Wynn was in fact the author of the first breed standard, as described in chapter 21 of his book, *The History of the Mastiff*, under the heading "The Points of the English Mastiff." Because he was rather influential for a period of time, Mr. Wynn is to blame for many of the faults that the breed carries still today, since he stub-bornly awarded the aforemen-tioned Crown Prince, whose nega-tive traits were spread by those who used him widely at stud. This same stubbornness regarding certain aspects caused Mr. Wynn to be despised and ridiculed by the Old English Mastiff Club (OEMC), founded in 1883, to such an extent that the OEMC leaders rejected his title of specialist judge.

FUNCTION OVER FORM

It was not esthetics but functionality that was considered the most deci-sive factor in the early days. The strongest dictated the rules. Everything depended on innate capacity to withstand and survive the harsh conditions imposed by nature or society.

The historical *Hutchinson's Dog Encyclopaedia,* published in the late 1920s, has become one of the most desirable volumes on dogs to collectors. This painting, rendered by F.T. Daws, was specially commissioned for that volume.

Today's Mastiff still possesses many of the features that were described in the first standard, though breeders have made considerable strides regarding soundness and consistency of type.

Similar to the politics that surround the world of pure-bred dogs today, the actual controversy was that, whether for good or bad, Mr. Wynn had "forgotten" to mention the OEMC in his book and had not included the "authorized" standard, written by the OEMC and accepted by

England's Kennel Club. Some things never change! Even so, the 222 pages of his book continue to be a treasure that offers an indispensable look at the tribulations that the ancestors of the modern Mastiff and his champions endured. In time, the OEMC succeeded in having its standard become the official one and, in the past 150 years, it has changed very little. With this standard, breeders finally reached a consensus on the desirable physical attributes of the Mastiff.

NEW DIFFICULTIES

Once breeders and the registry agreed upon the physical attributes of a pure-bred Mastiff, the breed's utility and purpose for being were challenged. It seems that there were very few uses for this dog since the banning of dog fighting. To worsen the situation for the giant Mastiff, a new breed was entering the picture. The Bullmastiff was viewed as a "substitute" for the breed, as this new breed was smaller framed and more agile than the Mastiff, from which it was bred down (of course, with crosses to the old Bulldog). The Bullmastiff was embraced by landowners and forest keepers seeking a guard dog, as well as by police corps.

History turned the screws tighter, and World War I made matters worse still. Due to their size and temperament, Mastiffs were difficult to keep, given the food shortages and the like. Many proud owners were forced to give up their majestic dogs. A few were then exported to the US, where there was a growing interest in the breed.

MASTIFFS IN AMERICA

There are but a few written references to Mastiffs in America; these were compiled by Norman Howard Carp-Gordon, of Mastiffs of Gordonshire, in his booklet *The Making of the Modern Mastiff*.

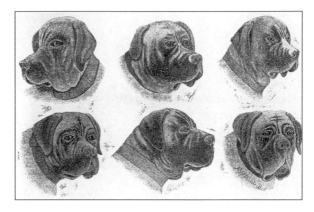

These references all point to the first white settlers who arrived in Massachusetts on board the Mayflower in 1620, carrying a

The breed in transition in the late 1800s—these important English dogs show the considerable variation in head type in the breed. They are: Hanbury's Duchess (1861), Field's Eng. Ch. King (1865), Eng. Ch. Turk (1867), Turner's Elaine (1883), Eng. Ch. Colonel (1873) and Eng. Ch. Pontiff (1879).

Enter the Bullmastiff, a breed composed of half-Bulldog and half-Mastiff, which became a "substitute" for the Mastiff because it was considered more agile and useful.

large "Mastiffe bitch." A man named Peter Browne owned this bitch, who seemed to have survived all difficulties and complications related to the boat trip, and all adjustments to the new lifestyle, and even attended the first Thanksgiving ceremony.

Another source explained how owners used dogs to defend themselves from attacks by the Native Americans. It was not until the end of the 19th century that the first Mastiffs were exhibited at dog shows. These first show exhibits appear to have been descendants of a pair of British dogs named Adam and Eve, which had been brought from England by Captain Garnier. This man settled down in Canada and later returned to England with a puppy from Adam and Eve named Lion.

Displaying the proper proportions for the Mastiff's head is the author's Neom des Chenaies Kom Pystou. How far we have come from the late 1800s!

While the Mastiff was undergoing difficult times in his homeland, the nearly extinct dog was becoming one of the most favored breeds in North America. American Kennel Club (AKC) statistics show that in 1890 the breed ranked fifth out of 37 recognized breeds, only outnumbered by Pointers, Setters, Collies and St. Bernards. In 1885, only 7 Mastiffs were registered in the AKC Stud Book, but 4 years later there were no fewer than 370 dogs registered, out of which 7 became champions in the US.

The Mastiff Club of America (MCA) was founded in 1929, and the first official standard of the breed was drafted and immediately approved by the AKC in the same year. Yet the breed's development on both sides of the Atlantic faced difficulties and was met with varying success through the 1940s. Dog breeders from all parts of the world cooperated with one another, despite the difficulties involved with transporting these large dogs by sea. The high costs of keeping a Mastiff in quarantine precluded most exportations of American

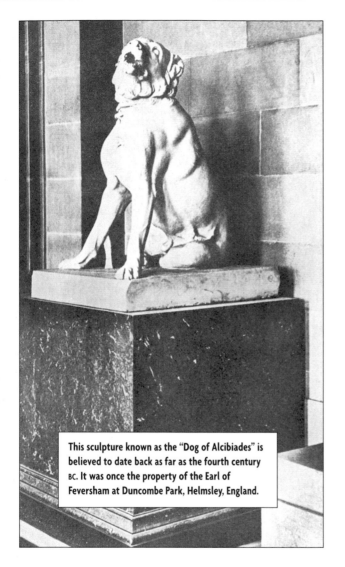

This sculpture known as the "Dog of Alcibiades" is believed to date back as far as the fourth century BC. It was once the property of the Earl of Feversham at Duncombe Park, Helmsley, England.

and those dogs who survived produced very few progeny to carry the breed into the next decade.

SAVING THE BREED

It is, however, precisely at difficult times that the strong come to the fore. The history of the Mastiff in the 20th century is a good example of that. When things got tough in Europe under the threat of German domination, many people left their homes and lands and ran away to the United States. Others who did not manage to make it did their best to send their dogs across the sea in a desperate attempt to preserve some lines and breeding programs, which in another way had been lost forever. American breeders mobilized to shelter as many "canine refugees" as possible. The dogs were transported to American territory in cargo ships.

The *Atlantic Journal Magazine* provides a detailed narration of the adventures lived by a pair of Mastiffs named Remus and Prunella. They had belonged to Frederick Bowles from Leicestershire, England

dogs to Britain. Of course, the 1940s were also complicated by World War II, which left the Mastiff in England in even worse condition; starvation pushed many owners and breeders to once more put their dogs down,

(Opposite Page)
Manuel Castellanos' "Patio de Caballos de la Plaza de Toros de Madrid," painted in 1853, shows ancient Mastiffs that are the forebears of our breed. This painting is on display at the famous Prado Museum in Madrid, Spain.

(today we have confirmed that both dogs were of the Mansatta affix). It was the King family in the city of Atlanta, Georgia who later took them in. In this report, dated August 11, 1940, author W. Neal tells how two enormous Mastiffs were given shelter in the house of Charles H. King's wife: "The two Mastiffs barely escaped the war." He went on to explain that due to the shortage of food in the UK that "they had to live on a diet of vegetable and toast, with the result that each of them had lost about 50 pounds, so they tipped the scales at a mere 150 apiece—only about five or six times as much as an ordinary dog weighs."

Neal also records Mrs. King's words on how many times she had written to the "five principal Mastiff breeders to know if they had dogs for sale. Four replied that they had done away with their kennels. The fifth, a Mr. Bowles, who lived near London,

said that he had put to sleep all but two of his finest pair of Mastiffs. They were named Remus and Prunella and he shipped them to me (...) About the time the dogs arrived, I received a letter from a famous dog show judge who suggested that I should try to find a Mastiff named Remus, the finest dog of its breed in the British Isles, he said. Since I already had Remus, this letter made me feel very happy."

All of this gives us an idea of the difficulties and hardships that English breeders went through and helps us to understand the necessity of their taking every possible step in the attempt to salvage the situation. Once the war was over, British dog fanciers knew that only a miracle could stop the breed from total extinction. The Old English Mastiff Club (OEMC) summoned all partners on October 25, 1946 for a meeting.

BULLMASTIFF TO THE RESCUE

At the beginning of World War II, there were 20 dogs under the British affix of Havengore, but the war's dramatic circumstances led them either to perish without leaving descendants or to be eventually sacrificed. Finally, a bitch named Sally of Coldblow, a descendant of Eng. Ch. Bill of Havengore, came to the rescue. She secured the breed's continuity after being mated with a brindle dog named Templecombe Taurus. Dog fanciers doubted if this dog was a pure Mastiff, a Mastiff/Bullmastiff cross or a pure Bullmastiff. In the end, they found out that he was an authentic Bullmastiff, but what mattered was that the breed had been saved from total extinction in its country of origin.

Fifteen people attended the meeting to discuss the crisis. The reality they faced was very disheartening. The few surviving dogs—seven in total—were too old to procreate. Therefore, it was decided that the club's secretary would travel to the United States to import dogs for the reconstruction of breeding programs. Unfortunately, she returned to England with empty hands, since there weren't many Mastiffs on the other side of the Atlantic either.

Luckily, a year later, two bitches from the affix of Heatherbelle were brought from Canada. They were the property of Mrs. Mellhuish. As the situation was so desperate, the OEMC decided that, for as long as it did not stabilize, all dogs born in the following years were to be registered under an "emergency" affix, which was no other than the club's own abbreviation by initials. The Kennel Club in England agreed, recognizing that desperate times require desperate measures.

However, there are still other significant facts that can't be forgotten if we are to truly understand the state of the breed after the war. These facts explain the need of using other breeds to "reconstruct" whatever little was still left of the Mastiff's legacy. These other two breeds were the Bullmastiff—a first cousin of the

MASTIFFS AROUND THE WORLD AT THE TURN OF THE 21ST CENTURY

AUSTRALIA	136
CANADA	264
FINLAND	8
FRANCE	69
GERMANY	50*
GREAT BRITAIN	528
IRELAND	5
ITALY	72
NEW ZEALAND	31
SPAIN	9
SOUTH AFRICAN REPUBLIC	8
SWEDEN	15
SWITZERLAND	1
UNITED STATES	5306

* The data from Germany exclusively refers to Mastiffs born in the country. Imported dogs are not included in VDH statistics. In the other cases, both dogs born in the mentioned countries as well as imported from others were included.

Mastiff—and the Dogue de Bordeaux of France.

Using the Bullmastiff to recover the Mastiff breed should not surprise us. The history and past of these two breeds have always been linked. They have been moving forward in time sometimes in unison, sometimes in parallel. However, that is not what people think of the Dogue de Bordeaux.

The powerful Dogue de Bordeaux, also known as the French Mastiff, was used in the reconstruction of the Mastiff, as was the Bullmastiff.

Mastiffs: first, with Weyacres Tasr; later, with Merle's Alvin. The two resulting litters set up the basis for a large number of American Mastiffs, born under different affixes (Bowats, Peach Farm, Heatherbelle, Rumblin, Havengore, Windhaven, etc.), which means that even today, a half-century later, there are still descendants from this "original sin"...a sin that served to refresh the blood and improve certain characteristics of the breed, which, due to high consanguinity (from the lack of fresh blood), had begun to generate serious health problems in dogs on both sides of the Atlantic.

Toward the middle of the 20th century, American dog breeder Merle Campbell imported a bitch with a legitimate pedigree from France. This bitch was registered in the French Stud Book as having been bred by Mr. Capel, who owned the Fenelon affix. She had been born on July 18, 1956 from a litter by French Ch. Xohor de Fenelon and the bitch Erine de Fenelon. Her name was Fidelle de Fenelon. What makes this of special mention is that this female left France with documents that identified her as a Dogue de Bordeaux, but was later registered with the American Kennel Club as a Mastiff!

Furthermore, some time later, the bitch was mated with two

This, in brief, is the extraordinary history and the hardships experienced by the Mastiff. The efforts made by a few people and the strength of the breed have allowed the Mastiff to survive to our day in spite of difficulties. Sydenham Edwards said about this beautiful animal in *Cynographia Britannica* in 1800, "The lion is to the cat, what the Mastiff to the dog. He is the noblest of the family. He stands alone, while the others kneel down before him..."

THE MASTIFF AROUND THE WORLD TODAY

At present and after so many years of hardship, the Mastiff seems finally able to face the future in a positive way. Although the breed is still relatively not very popular worldwide, dog breeders working on its improvement do it with a sense of responsibility; they are aware of the importance of keeping the breed alive.

Curiously, and in spite of originating in Britain, it is in the United States where the Mastiff has the largest number of fanciers and breeders. A large variety of breeding programs and lines also allow a wider genetic pool in this country, which explains why the United States is currently leading the Mastiff's breeding in the world. This does not mean that the work carried out in its country of origin as well as in countries like Germany, Holland and France— although on a minor scale— should be underestimated.

Int. Ch. Logan de la Tivoliere and Novak, showing off their tremendous size and good looks while posing with a trio of handsome Spanish horses.

Any ordinary person, upon meeting you walking your Mastiff on the street, would most likely feel the urge to move aside and let you both pass. He might even consider crossing to the other side of the street "just in case." The Mastiff's imposing presence, tremendous size, enormous head and voluminous body instill respect and a degree of fear into most reasonable individuals. Yet, to those who own and love the Mastiff, what is most astounding is that beneath the breed's impressive exterior is a tender, sensitive being who is serene and quiet. He is confident about his strength and power and knows that his appearance makes humans notice him.

DOES A MASTIFF SUIT YOUR LIFESTYLE?

Before we further explore the breed's temperament, let's pause for a moment to consider the responsibility that you are undertaking by adopting a Mastiff. Many dog lovers are so enamored of the giant Mastiff that they forget how large a dog he is and what requirements he demands. And when a Mastiff demands something, you'd better be ready to listen and provide!

The very size that makes the Mastiff so attractive and spectacular also places demands on the owner. That same awesome appearance is accompanied by *at least* 120 pounds and 27.5 inches at the withers (and that's for the smallest female!). Although the AKC does not specify weight in its breed standard, females usually range from 120–170 lb, and males from 160–230 lb. That means that even if you think of a tender three-month-old puppy, you are envisioning an animal that weighs some 40 lb or more! It won't be easy to hold a Mastiff pup in your arms if he gets tired after a walk through the countryside or the city, or if he gets sick.

The dog's size also places demands on your choice of vehicle. An adult Mastiff does not fit into your two-door BMW. You will need to buy a large sports utility vehicle or van to accommodate your 150-lb-plus chum. Likewise, because Mastiffs are rather clumsy (truth be told!), you

Int. Ch. Night Stalker REO Speed Wagon is known as Titan, and at one year of age he is taller than his owner, Lisa Edwards-Filu.

will need to have a ramp to help the dog climb into the vehicle. This is not a graceful animal!

In your home, the dog will require several comfortable places to rest. You want these places to be out of the way, not near hallways, drafts or any electrical appliances, as the electromagnetic waves are harmful to his health. If you live in a small apartment, space may be a demand you cannot meet. I'm not saying that it will be impossible, only that it will not be convenient or easy.

One solution could be sharing the sofa with your Mastiff. However, if you decide to do this, you must realize that your three-month old puppy, in about three or four months, will take up more of the sofa than you do...and soon there will be no room for you at all! You will have to move to the floor or purchase a larger or second sofa.

Then there is that glorious slobber! You must also consider your laundry bills. Mastiffs like to be a part of the family, so your dog wants to be a part of your home life every possible moment. For example, when you are dressed up for church or the office, your Mastiff will want to give you a moist "good-morning" kiss. You can be certain that you will become your dry cleaner's favorite person! Expect that your laundry expenses will be higher than those of your pre-Mastiff life.

Another new expense to consider is the veterinarian. You need to find a vet who understands the needs of large-breed dogs. This is imperative to your dog's continued health. Mastiff puppies need to see the vet every 15 days! Since the breed is prone to radical growth spurts, it is advisable to have the vet supervise these as closely as possible. Your Mastiff puppy, whose newborn weight was a mere 1.5 lb, will multiply that weight almost a hundredfold before reaching one year of age. Such dramatic weight gain has an impact on your puppy's growing limbs and muscles, and your veterinarian must know how to handle these growing pains.

Your vet will also perform regular check-ups on your dog, including x-rays and blood tests to determine if the puppy suffers from any of the hereditary problems that affect the Mastiff breed. Some of the problems can be corrected surgically, though they render your dog worthless for breeding purposes. Discuss the potential problems with your chosen breeder before purchasing your pup. Of course, your breeder should have screened his stock for hereditary problems before planning the mating.

Don't let all of this discourage you from deciding on a Mastiff puppy. You can hope that you will encounter none of these problems with your Mastiff, but it's always better to err on the side of knowledge and caution. Be prepared for the worst, and hope for the best. Keep in mind that your pup's welfare is entirely in your hands. You own him and his life, so be responsible when taking on such an enormous role in another creature's life.

THE GENTLE GIANT'S TEMPERAMENT

In just two words, I can sum up the Mastiff thusly: gentle giant. The Mastiff is a self-confident dog that knows he is powerful and never acts without provocation or reason. Mastiffs seem to assess a given situation before acting, carefully evaluating the factors before making a move.

This is a family dog who really needs to feel like an "insider" in your home. He is not independent like other molosser breeds. He likes to be in the company of his owner and feels a particular liking toward children, of whom he is keenly protective.

This young lady is very well protected by her massive baby-sitter. The gentle giant guarantees that no harm will come to his family members.

Mastiffs get used to living outdoors only if there is no other choice. However, owners who make this decision miss most of the wonders that accompany sharing life with such a majestic, intelligent creature. The reader can trust my words. When the Mastiff is involved in the family life, he is serene, docile and able to give humans the best of himself.

Not only for the Mastiff's "feelings" but also for your own protection, it is vital to make this powerful dog feel like an integral part of your home and family. You cannot expect your Mastiff to defend your home and property if he doesn't feel attached to it. A Mastiff will only raise a paw for those with whom he has a profound relationship of respect, admiration and love.

Our gentle giant is quiet and extremely sensible. He prefers a loving stroke, a kind word or an appreciative look more than any tidbit or treat. Physical contact means a lot to him, just like proximity to "his" family. That is why it is so cruel not to include him in the home with the family and to relegate him to isolation in the backyard or a kennel run.

The history of the Mastiff speaks well of this extraordinarily brave dog, which is capable of fighting and defeating wild beasts. But those were other times—times when, because of the prevailing circumstances and cultures, the

A rock star in the making? The Mastiff lets his playful side shine through around his close friends.

Mastiff was not given the opportunity to show his true gentle nature. What else could be expected from an animal that was kept chained for most of his lifetime? Even today we know—and canine therapists have dealt with many such cases—of dogs, regardless of their breed, size or condition, that are still kept in extreme isolation and are tortured by their limited mobility. They end up suffering from serious behavioral disorders, extensive trauma and aggressiveness. It is thus not surprising that the Mastiff of the past was very different from that of modern times.

Maybe a good way to describe his behavior could be this self-explanatory anecdote. Let us imagine one of these giant dogs lying comfortably on the floor and relaxing happily. The owner passes by, carrying a huge pile of books, and accidentally trips and drops the books on top of the dog. They fall noisily to the floor. Many (and I mean *many*) seconds later, the Mastiff, without much bother, looks at his owner as if to say, "Are you finished?"

An onlooker, who does not know the Mastiff's temperament, might well think the dog a dull, semi-conscious lump. Misjudging the dog, the person could think that the dog is slow, foolish and queerly disinterested in his surroundings. It is true that the

Mastiff is not "alert" in the usual canine sense of the word, the way a terrier or spaniel is ready to spring into action. Nonetheless, this same Mastiff who would not pass standard "temperament tests" moves at his own peculiar pace, smartly assessing the situation before moving into action. The Mastiff is as powerful and deliberate as he is intuitive and profound. This dog possesses the innate capacity to decide whether or not his intervention (power, strength, boldness) are required in a given situation. How many jumpy spaniels or hyperactive terriers can lay claim to that ability?

The author must confess, however, that this same brilliant dog does suffer from a somewhat unique "disorder," which I jokingly refer to as "Selective Hearing Disorder." I am not talking about an anomaly of the auditory system. It is simply that when you give your Mastiff a command, he very deliberately takes his time in "deciding" if this a good time to obey your "request."

Sensitivity is another of the Mastiff's special traits. The Mastiff is keenly in tune to his master, knowing a person's feelings and reacting to them in a surprisingly human way. If you are sad, he is the first to approach you with a sympathetic tongue. If you are in pain, he will stay unobtrusively by your side, as if trying to

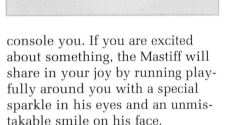

BATTLING THE LION

Discretion is the Mastiff's banner. That is why he rarely barks. His mere size makes his potential foes shudder. The Mastiff is not wicked, either. He will openly avoid confronting other animals, except when the life of his family or his own life is at stake. The Mastiff is unbeatable, so fighting this giant that can be well over 200 lb is useless—he will always win. Consider this: "The Mastiff is to the dog what the lion is to the cat." Do you want to battle a lion?

console you. If you are excited about something, the Mastiff will share in your joy by running playfully around you with a special sparkle in his eyes and an unmistakable smile on his face.

These special qualities enable the Mastiff to get under our skin; to know us much better than we know ourselves. Thus, our dog is able to manipulate us at every turn, skillfully working to get his way in all matters. Be wary to make sure that your Mastiff doesn't succeed in ruling your kingdom and becoming the lion of your pride (in this case, your family "pack").

GUARDING INSTINCT
The first-time or potential owner usually asks what kind of specific training is needed to ensure that his Mastiff will

A 600-pound wall of protection! Who could doubt that this child has anything less than a professional security system?

By definition, instinct is an animal's innate fixed pattern of behavior in response to certain stimuli, often associated with the survival or preservation of the animal's species. Nature provides the instinct for all creatures to defend themselves from harm or potential threat. In the Mastiff, this instinct—to protect or guard—is natural and does not need to be taught, though training can help hone or improve the natural ability of the dog.

And how do we improve it? By allowing the Mastiff into our pack and letting him know that he belongs to a social group made up of family members (spouses, children, grandparents, other pets, etc.). This is the best way to nurture the Mastiff's protective instincts.

Those who attempt to train a Mastiff for guarding and defense using the traditional training methods, such as Schutzhund, for instance, are wasting their time and money. They will probably end up destroying the Mastiff's excellent temperament and turning him into what he is not: an aggressive, intolerant animal with whom coexistence becomes unbearable.

develop into a competent guard dog. To this inevitable question, the author says, absolutely none beyond basic obedience. You must commit seriously to the training of the puppy, including proper socialization and the enforcement of every house rule. You must be clear with the puppy from the first day, showing him exactly how to behave in every situation, what is right and wrong, what is acceptable and forbidden. Every family member must adhere to the same way of training and instructing. That is the only secret. Once the Mastiff understands his place in your home, as well as who is boss and his "sits" and "stays," he naturally will take on the added responsibility of protecting his home and family. Instinctively, he will protect you.

BEHAVIOR WITH STRANGERS
The Mastiff likes to feel useful and needs his family members to trust in his ability to protect them. He performs his duty with no

fanfare and expects no rewards for his service. When the Mastiff is with any one of his family members, he is calm, playful and sensitive. With strangers, he is distant and distrusting. His tact does not force him to pretend to be otherwise. He will observe the visitor from a prudent distance, as if he is analyzing pros and cons, or mentally calculating the space separating them. In most cases, he will not approach the stranger, even if the owner insists.

The frequent visitor to the family's home will admit over and over again that the family dog does not welcome him very effusively, or, worse, the dog does not welcome him at all. If the Mastiff finally does take to the stranger, it is due to the dog's decision to like the person for some special reason. If the dog does not like the person, he will keep away as long as the visitor stays and as many times as he comes. This is typical of the Mastiff, whose ancestors were not known to be welcoming to strangers: *Cave canum*—beware the dog!

However, the disinterested Mastiff is not the same as a barking aggressive dog who dislikes everyone. As the owner of a Mastiff, it's important for you to understand that an aggressive barking dog is *not* a better guardian. Such a dog lacks socialization and self-confidence. A properly reared Mastiff has no

TAKING CARE

Science is showing that as people take care of their pets, the pets are taking care of their owners. A study published in the *American Journal of Cardiology* found that having a pet can prolong his owner's life. Pet owners generally have lower blood pressure, and pets help their owners to relax and keep more physically fit. It was also found that pets help to keep the elderly connected to their communities.

reason to lunge and bark at strangers—he knows he's king and there's no need to shout about it. Again, this underlines the impor-

The Mastiff is not the most active breed you could choose, though it's hard to find a better chum to take a snooze with.

tance of socializing the puppy and exposing him to the outdoors, other dogs and strangers. All of your efforts will contribute positively to shaping his temperament and making a confident, dependable companion and protector.

MALE VERSUS FEMALE

While the male is more substantial in size and overall bulk, both genders are very large animals, with the dogs often surpassing 200 lbs and bitches 150 lbs. Height at the withers is over 30 inches for males and over 27.5 inches for females. The average person won't be able to distinguish a male from a female at a single glance even though bitches are rather smaller and lighter than dogs. In most cases, females have less bone and it is rather expected that they look, with a few exceptions, more "feminine." Males and females

are not much different in temperament and behavior, but it is true that hormones play a definitive role in certain aspects of attitude and development.

The bitch's reproductive system is, indeed, very different from that of the dog. That can be appreciated at first sight. They have a double row—nearly even—of mammary glands and nipples that grow with their physical maturity and especially after they have completed their first heat. The vulva is not easily distinguishable during puppyhood and puberty since it is hidden in the inner thighs, but it enlarges during and after the heat, at which time a bitch's behavior and attitude also are different.

We know that hormones are body secretions, which are released by certain organs and transported by blood circulation. They excite, inhibit and/or regulate the activities of other organs or organ systems in the body. In this case, sexual hormones play a directly or indirectly significant role, which can be expressed through behavior, attitude or

DROOL AND DRIBBLE
Like other bull-and-mastiff breeds, Mastiffs tend to drool and dribble, particularly after drinking. Dogs also salivate to control body temperature. It is always sensible to keep a drool cloth handy!

LOOK OUT!
Mastiffs tend to be rather clumsy and knock things over, primarily because they seem to be unaware of how big they are. A Mastiff is quite capable of knocking over a child or an adult, albeit without malice.

temperament. These hormones are also involved in setting up the differences for height, weight, external appearance and the femininity or masculinity of each animal.

Furthermore, sexual hormones determine not only the speed at which each dog will reach the peak of his sexual behavior but also when he will reach psychological and physical maturity. Maturity in the Mastiff, both psychological and physical, comes rather late, both in dogs and bitches. Sexual maturity in both usually comes around six or eight months of age, which is long before physical maturity is reached at about two to three years of age.

This is a very important fact that should be taken into account. Breeders should never allow their bitches to mate until they are two years of age at the very least. Likewise, in the case of dogs, breeders should not put a Mastiff to stud on a regular basis much sooner than two years of age. While their sexual organs are fully grown, the dog's skeletal and muscular systems are still developing and are not ready to bear the stress of such physical activities.

Any pediatrician, or even experienced parents, can tell you that girls mature faster than boys. The same happens with Mastiffs. Bitches seem to mature before dogs do, and they learn faster. Males always seem to travel in the

This bitch displays the typical loyal expression of the female Mastiff.

back seat. They are always late and spend a few more months manifesting childish behavior, which rather contradicts their great size.

Not knowing about the dogs' late-coming maturity can make new owners believe that their enormous dogs are somewhat mentally slow, especially if compared to a German Shepherd, a Collie or even a Yorkshire Terrier of the same chronological age. Dog breeders should be patient and understand that the Mastiff's biological time clock is slower, but his mind is no less sharp than that of another breed.

Mastiffs have been listed in the *Guinness Book of World Records* for being the largest dogs in the world. At the end of the 1980s, Alcama Zorba of La Susa registered almost 57 inches of thoracic perimeter and 37 inches at the withers, and weighed 343 lb. Murphy followed him, weighing 293 lb, with 53 inches of thoracic perimeter and standing 35 inches at the withers.

HARMONY BETWEEN THE SEXES
The author recommends that a new owner who wishes to own only one Mastiff select a bitch. This is especially so if the new owner intends to use his Mastiff for companionship and protection. Usually, after her first heat (at around 8–12 months of age), her protective natural instinct will be already developed for guard work. She will show these protective instincts, but only when necessary.

If possible, the author recommends that owners consider adopting more than one Mastiff, providing that the owner's home, property and budget allow for such an undertaking. The ideal would be getting the bitch first, then waiting until she is 6 or 8 months old (better yet, 10 or 12 months old) to bring in a dog. That is the best time to bring the dog in, as at that time the bitch will be ready to "teach" her partner everything that she has already learned. And besides, while the dog grows, he will be

SPAYING BITCHES
Spaying reduces a bitch's risk of suffering from reproductive cancers, though the incidence varies depending on the procedure elected by the veterinarian and owner and on the age of the bitch. Bitches spayed by means of an ovarian hysterectomy have only a 1% risk of suffering from any kind of tumor in the reproductive system. For bitches spayed by complete extirpation of the uterus and the ovaries during the time between the first and second cycle, the risk increases to 10%. For bitches spayed over two years of age, the risk increases to 25%; in bitches over four or five years of age, the risk is more than 50%.

Four generations of quality Mastiffs, left to right: Taboo at eleven years old; Ch. Pluto at seven-and-a-half years old; Spike at two years old and winning in the show ring; and Cassie at one year old.

getting a sense of ownership over his bitch, which could speed up his maturation process.

While this may sound like a nice scenario, owning a pair of Mastiffs certainly could complicate home matters, such as having to keep them separated when the bitch is "in heat" to avoid unwanted pregnancy. Of course, such problems can be eliminated by spaying the female/neutering the male (or both), which is recommended for all pet dogs. Besides softening the dog's temperament, neutering can also prevent him (or her, if spaying a bitch) from suffering from serious health problems. For this reason alone, this surgical procedure is a

smart decision for pet owners not interested in showing or breeding Mastiffs.

The temperament and behavior of male dogs are not as "altered" by neutering as the temperament and behavior of bitches that are spayed. Neutering a dog eliminates the possibility of testicular cancer and lessens the risk of prostate cancer, especially if the dog has never been used at stud, after he is six or seven years old. Spaying has similar health benefits for females, preventing or reducing the risk of certain cancers and other problems.

Another possibility for the multi-Mastiff home would be adopting two or more bitches.

Many people have fallen into the trap of wanting to adopt more than one Mastiff once they have enjoyed the company of their first. Since the breed is quite gregarious with one another, such a scenario is not impossible—costly, time- and space-consuming and, possibly, a little maddening—but not impossible. The breed is non-combative, as you would expect, given its confident air and power. Mastiffs are very tolerant of one another and not given to fights. They accept and respect one another and, at the same time, they tolerate most other pets. This general rule certainly does not apply to Mastiffs that have not been properly socialized or that suffer from excessive shyness.

So, yes, I say that owning a herd of Mastiffs is possible, but, nevertheless, I personally do not advise it, especially for inexperienced owners. If the new owner wishes to obtain a second Mastiff, after unmistakable success with his first (a bitch), then adopting a male is my strong recommendation. Yet when dealing with around 400 lb of dog (the weight of two Mastiffs), the devil should not be tempted!

A FRIEND FOR LIFE

In 1891, William Wade said, regarding how Mastiffs should be taught, "To anyone who wishes to rear a true Mastiff, in all his perfection of utility, let me say, begin by making a friend of your dog, let him accompany you on your walks abroad; let him come into your house and lie before your fire and in every way connect himself with you and your well-being (...) Do not attempt to 'conquer' him or 'break him in' (...) First love your dog, next make him love you; you will never regret having gained his love and confidence, and the day may come when you will be repaid an hundredfold."

Harsh words, threats, shouts, ill treatment and punishment only make the Mastiff lose interest in and respect for his master. It is consistency and repetition that teach the Mastiff to understand what is right and wrong. That is why it is so important, from the first day, that all people living under the same roof with a Mastiff know well what will be and will not be permitted of the dog in the future. All family members should also be equally involved in teaching the dog. What is white will continue to be white forever, and what is black will be black. Gray tones are meaningless. Consistency is the key. It is that simple. There is a saying that summarizes this quite well: "Mastiffs need loving friends, not just owners." That is the truth.

While breeders do not recommend that you encourage your Mastiff to jump like this because of potential harm to the dog's orthopedic health, it sure is impressive that this giant dog can be so agile.

BREED STANDARD FOR THE

MASTIFF

A breed standard is essentially a "word picture," describing the ideal specimen of a breed. It is used by breeders and judges to determine which dogs live up to the standard (and thus conform to it) and which dogs do not (and therefore should not be used for breeding). I personally feel the breed standard to be the "bible" by which every credible breeder abides. Since the standard is subject to each breeder's (and judge's) interpretation, there can be differing opinions as to what is correct, desired or acceptable. Thus, it is not uncommon to see dogs in the same breed ring differing greatly in type, substance and size. This is particularly so with the Mastiff and the other molossers. You only need to attend a dog show to notice it. Sadly, you will see for yourself that every breeder has interpreted the standard in accordance with his or her own tastes or preferences, instead of abiding strictly by the standard.

Douglas B. Oliff explained it well when he said, "The interpretation of a breed standard is often

a personal one. It is always possible for different individuals to read different meanings or emphasis into the same words. All that one hopes for is that everyone studies the standard and formulates an opinion on what it is attempting to say. A far greater appreciation will be achieved if one knows why the requirements were made in the first place."

When M.B. Wynn defined, in 1886, the general characteristics of Mastiffs, he was prophetic. He said that "vast dogs long on the legs, somewhat light in bone for their size, are not in reality Mastiffs, whatever their owners may think." This is still valid today, even in the 21st century, the third millennium!

The first official standard of the Mastiff breed was written more than 100 years ago. Little in it has been changed since then, generally speaking. The standard of the Fédération Cynologique Internationale (FCI), which is used in most European and Latin American countries, is almost a literal translation of the British standard. However, American and

At dog shows, the judge uses the breed standard to determine which dog most closely conforms to the description set forth in that official document. It is this dog that takes home first place, as Ch. Fearnought the Barbarian is proudly doing here.

Canadian fanciers have made some significant changes, while enthusiasts from Australia and New Zealand, who currently use the British standard, are considering making some changes.

The head, one of the Mastiff's most distinctive traits, should not be exaggerated, as this could offset the dog's balance and movement. Unfortunately, currently a large number of dog breeders and fanciers puts too much emphasis on the head. In my opinion, this is misguided, as breeders must focus on the dog as an harmonious whole. We do not want to destroy the Mastiff's balance and transform him into a big-headed, useless monster!

The Mastiff's legs should be firm, with moderate angulation, and his feet should be rounded and well arched. As Dee Dee Anderson cleverly puts it: "I guarantee those knights in former times did not carry the Mastiffs on horseback to get to the battle site." It is clear that our modern Mastiffs should continue to be capable of great activity whenever called upon, though they remain quiet, peaceful beings who love to recline on a comfy sofa.

Agility is a requirement for the active guard dog; the Mastiff attacks his opponent, when he needs to, by physically knocking him down. To do that, he needs to be agile enough to move his whole body forward and support himself standing upright on his hind legs. Unfortunately, most dogs today are excessively heavy, and their hindquarters are so weak and poorly conditioned that such a feat would be next to impossible. They end up with their buttocks on the ground or, in worst cases, with patellar or ligament injuries. This sad state of affairs is a result of breeders' exaggerating the Mastiff's rear angulation, trying to make the Mastiff's hindquarters resemble those of the Boxer or German Shepherd—another woefully misguided notion that some breeders have embraced.

By studying the standard, we come to see that the Mastiff is intended to be a solid, well-built dog with a strong, agile body. Such a dog need not have excessive size or weight.

Let's also discuss temperament, which is described in the standard along with the Mastiff's ideal physical characteristics and movement. This is a brave, intelligent and self-confident dog. He trusts his family and friends and distrusts strangers, just the way it should be. However, we should not take distrust for shyness. The shy dog is the one that sticks his tail between his legs and carries his head low. His face indicates his fear and he can actually bite someone if cornered. None of these traits characterizes the Mastiff. The standard is very precise regarding this aspect. When we face a well-balanced Mastiff, we are looking at a quiet, confident animal whose integrity and confidence cannot be compromised by a threatening stranger.

THE AMERICAN KENNEL CLUB STANDARD FOR THE MASTIFF

General Appearance: The Mastiff is a large, massive, symmetrical dog with a well-knit frame. The impression is one of grandeur and dignity. Dogs are more massive throughout. Bitches should not be faulted for being somewhat smaller in all dimensions while maintaining a proportionally powerful structure. A good evaluation considers positive qualities of type and soundness with equal weight.

Size, Proposition, Substance: *Size*—Dogs, minimum, 30 inches at the shoulder. Bitches, minimum, 27 inches at the shoulder. *Fault*—Dogs or bitches below the minimum standard. The farther below standard, the greater the fault. *Proportion*—Rectangular, the length of the dog from forechest to rump is somewhat longer than the height at the withers. The height of the dog should come from depth of body rather than from length of leg. *Substance*—Massive, heavy boned, with a powerful muscle structure. Great depth and breadth desirable. *Fault*—Lack of substance or slab sided.

Head: In general outline giving a massive appearance when viewed from any angle. Breadth greatly desired. *Eyes* set wide apart, medium in size, never too prominent. *Expression* alert but kindly. Color of eyes brown, the darker the better, and showing no haw. Light eyes or a predatory expression is undesirable. *Ears* small in proportion to the skull, V-shaped, rounded at the tips. Leather moderately thin, set widely apart at the highest points on the sides of the skull continuing the outline across the summit. They should lie close to the cheeks when in repose. Ears dark in color, the blacker the better, conforming to the color of the muzzle.

Skull broad and somewhat flattened between the ears, forehead slightly curved, showing marked wrinkles which are particularly distinctive when at attention. Brows (superciliary ridges) moderately raised. Muscles of the temples well developed, those of the cheeks extremely powerful. Arch across the skull a flattened curve with a furrow up the center of the forehead. This extends from between the eyes to halfway up the skull. The *stop* between the eyes well marked but not too abrupt. *Muzzle* should be half the

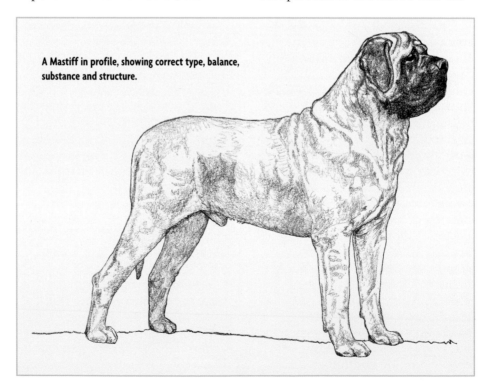

A Mastiff in profile, showing correct type, balance, substance and structure.

length of the skull, thus dividing the head into three parts—one for the foreface and two for the skull. In other words, the distance from the tip of the nose to stop is equal to one-half the distance between the stop and the occiput. Circumference of the muzzle (measured midway between the eyes and nose) to that of the head (measured before the ears) is as 3 is to 5.

Muzzle short, broad under the eyes and running nearly equal in width to the end of the nose. Truncated, i.e. blunt and cut off square, thus forming a right angle with the upper line of the face. Of great depth from the point of the nose to the underjaw. Underjaw broad to the end and slightly rounded. Muzzle dark in color, the blacker the better. *Fault* snipiness of the muzzle.

Nose broad and always dark in color, the blacker the better, with spread flat nostrils (not pointed or turned up) in profile. *Lips* diverging at obtuse angles with the septum and sufficiently pendulous so as to show a modified square profile. *Canine Teeth* healthy and wide apart. Jaws powerful. Scissors bite preferred, but a moderately undershot jaw should not be faulted providing the teeth are not visible when the mouth is closed.

Neck, Topline, Body: *Neck* powerful, very muscular, slightly arched, and of medium length.

Mastiff head study, showing correct type in this important feature of the breed.

The neck gradually increases in circumference as it approaches the shoulder. Neck moderately "dry" (not showing an excess of loose skin). *Topline*—In profile the topline should be straight, level, and firm, not swaybacked, roached, or dropping off sharply behind the high point of the rump.

Chest wide, deep, rounded, and well let down between the forelegs, extending at least to the elbow. Forechest should be deep and well defined with the breastbone extending in front of the foremost point of the shoulders. Ribs well rounded. False ribs deep and well set back. *Underline*—There should be a reasonable, but not exaggerated,

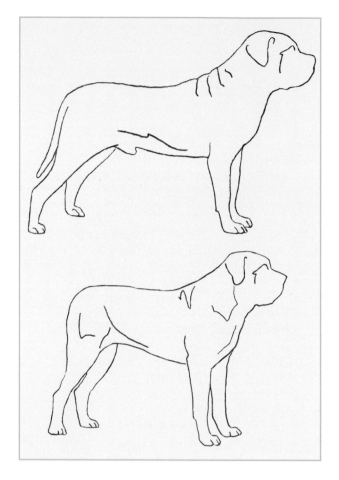

Forequarters: *Shoulders* moderately sloping, powerful and muscular, with no tendency to looseness. Degree of front angulation to match correct rear angulation. *Legs* straight, strong and set wide apart, heavy boned. *Elbows* parallel to body. *Pasterns* strong and bent only slightly. *Feet* large, round, and compact with well arched toes. Black nails preferred.

Hindquarters: *Hindquarters* broad, wide and muscular. *Second thighs* well developed, leading to a strong hock joint. *Stifle joint* is moderately angulated matching the front. *Rear legs* are wide apart and parallel when viewed from the rear. When the portion of the leg below the hock is correctly "set back" and stands perpendicular to the ground, a plumb line dropped from the rearmost point of the hindquarters will pass in front of the foot. This rules out straight hocks, and since stifle angulation varies with hock angulation, it also rules out insufficiently angulated stifles. *Fault*—Straight stifles.

tuck-up. Back muscular, powerful, and straight. When viewed from the rear, there should be a slight rounding over the rump. *Loins* wide and muscular.

    Tail set on moderately high and reaching to the hocks or a little below. Wide at the root, tapering to the end, hanging straight in repose, forming a slight curve, but never over the back when the dog is in motion.

Coat: Outer coat straight, coarse, and of moderately short length. Undercoat dense, short, and close lying. Coat should not be so long as to produce "fringe" on the belly, tail, or hind legs. *Fault* Long or wavy coat.

Color: Fawn, apricot, or brindle. Brindle should have fawn or apricot as a background color which should be completely covered with very dark stripes. Muzzle, ears, and nose must be dark in color, the blacker the better, with similar color tone around the eye orbits and extending upward between them. A small patch of white on the chest is permitted.

Faults—Excessive white on the chest or white on any other part of the body. Mask, ears, or nose lacking dark pigment.

Gait: The gait denotes power and strength. The rear legs should have drive, while the forelegs should track smoothly with good reach. In motion, the legs move straight forward; as the dog's speed increases from a walk to a trot, the feet move in toward the center line of the body to maintain balance.

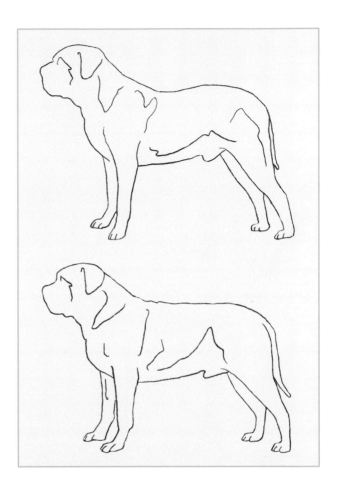

MEETING THE IDEAL
The American Kennel Club defines a standard as: "A description of the ideal dog of each recognized breed, to serve as an ideal against which dogs are judged at shows." This "blueprint" is drawn up by the breed's recognized parent club, approved by a majority of its membership and then submitted to the AKC for approval. The AKC states that "An understanding of any breed must begin with its standard. This applies to all dogs, not just those intended for showing."

Temperament: A combination of grandeur and good nature, courage and docility. Dignity, rather than gaiety, is the Mastiff's correct demeanor. Judges should not condone shyness or viciousness. Conversely, judges should also beware of putting a premium on showiness.

Approved November 12, 1991
Effective December 31, 1991

Faults in profile. (Top dog) Upright shoulders, weak front, toes out, dip behind shoulders, roach over loin, straight in rear, lacking in angulation. (Bottom dog) Low on leg, heavy-bodied but lacking bone in legs, weak pasterns, flat feet.

MASTIFF

SELECTING A PUPPY

Once you have decided that you are willing to share an important part of your life with this wonderful breed, then comes the time to find your ideal Mastiff friend. The first and most important thing is to relax—this is not a race. All good things take time. It is likewise indispensable to gather as much information as possible on the breed and its characteristics by reading, attending dog shows and meeting experienced owners and breeders to exchange ideas. Mastiff people are always willing to recommend responsible breeders and to steer you away from unworthy sources of puppies.

Attending dog shows is also a good opportunity to make contacts with the breed clubs, local, regional or national, and to observe the dogs at the show in competition. Unfortunately, there is considerable variation in type in the show ring, and you will have to decide which kennels have the kind of dogs that you think most correctly exemplify the breed standard or the kind of dogs that you prefer.

Once you have made contact with the breeder(s) you like, you then will have the opportunity to visit, to see the kennel facilities,

TEMPERAMENT COUNTS

Your selection of a good puppy can be determined by your needs. A show potential or a good pet? It is your choice. Every puppy, however, should be of good temperament. Although show-quality puppies are bred and raised with emphasis on physical conformation, responsible breeders strive for equally good temperament. Do not buy from a breeder who concentrates solely on physical beauty at the expense of personality.

to meet the pups and adult dogs, etc. Getting to know your puppy's breeder is essential to your puppy's future. You will want to remain in touch with the breeder to help you sort out all of the small dilemmas that you may encounter as your Mastiff pup grows up. We cannot forget that a puppy is a living being with feelings and needs. The Mastiff needs to have a close relationship with his owner, so choosing the right breeder with healthy, well-socialized, properly bred and lovingly reared puppies is no small matter. To an extent, the next 10 to 14 years of life with your Mastiff depend on how well you choose the breeder.

In most countries, Mastiffs are not as popular as a lot of the other

At about five weeks of age, these puppies are ready to meet potential owners, though they will not be ready to leave for their new homes for another few weeks.

breeds! Finding a good breeder will take some time and effort, as there are not that many serious breeders. Any responsible breeder has a very conscientious breeding program, based on experience and concrete expectations. Usually, he does not have puppies for sale throughout the whole year. Distrust any breeder who turns a puppy sale into a mere financial transaction, even if he is the only one with a puppy for sale in the dead of winter. The quality and soundness of the breed are not as important to this breeder as making a profit.

When dealing with your breeder, you will most likely be subject to a lengthy scrutiny. This is the sign that the breeder is a true lover of the breed, committed to the welfare of his puppies, someone who looks after his dogs with his whole heart and soul. The breeder may ask you to fill out a question-naire prior to anything else and,

"YOU BETTER SHOP AROUND!"

Finding a reputable breeder who sells healthy pups is very important, but make sure that the breeder you choose is not only someone you respect but also someone with whom you feel comfortable. Your breeder will be a resource long after you buy your puppy, and you must be able to call with reasonable questions with-out being made to feel like a pest! If you don't connect on a personal level, investigate some other breeders before making a final decision.

if you agree to buy a puppy from him and he agrees to sell you one, he will also ask you to sign a contract.

You may also have to be placed on a waiting list for a puppy. This is common practice with most good breeders, especially those of the less common breeds. Likewise, the breeder should give you references to other owners of his puppies, who are, of course, happy clients who live with sound, healthy Mastiff friends. If you have chosen a good breeder, these contacts will undoubtedly tell you how very worth the wait the breeder's puppies are!

Potential Mastiff owners should also be well advised of the inherited health concerns that have been documented in the breed. Most, if not all, breeds of pure-bred dog these days have to contend with hereditary conditions, for which all responsible breeders screen in order to eliminate the problems from their lines. The breeder you choose should have a spotless reputation. Such a breeder will test his potential sires and dams to ensure that they do not pass certain defects on to their offspring. They will also test puppies to make sure they are not carriers of these diseases. Among the diseases for which Mastiff breeders screen are: progressive retinal atrophy (PRA), cistinuria, hip and elbow dysplasia, retinal dysplasia, entropion, lung stenosis, sub-aortic stenosis, hypothyroidism, persistent pupillary membrane, osteochondritis dissecans (OCD) and Wobbler syndrome.

The latest veterinary research reveals that hip dysplasia (HD) elbow dysplasia (ED), OCD and other types of bone malformation are not exclusively hereditary in origin. These also can be direct

PUPPY APPEARANCE

Your puppy should have a well-fed appearance but not a distended abdomen, which may indicate worms or incorrect feeding, or both. The body should be firm, with a solid feel. The skin of the abdomen should be pale pink and clean, without signs of scratching or rash.

consequences of malnutrition, excessive calcium supply and high-protein food during the growing stages. A direct relation has also been found between the abuse of certain food additives, such as BHA, BHT, Etoxiquin and others, and the development of these diseases. This would explain why, after many years of controlling hip dysplasia by removing affected dogs from breeding programs, many young dogs, descendants of strictly controlled lines, are still diagnosed with HD.

It may also indicate why, in the past, when Mastiffs were fed fresh food (before the age of commercial food), such diseases were practically unknown. Those breeders who refuse to acknowledge the direct correlation between these prepared diets and

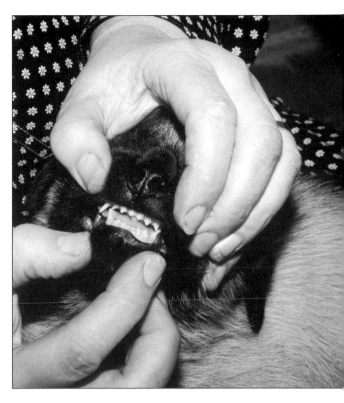

certain orthopedic conditions (elbow and hip dysplasia, OCD and panosteitis) will never eradicate the problems from their lines without abandoning commercial foods. Some experts also believe that there is likely a direct relationship between these diets and many allergies that are becoming serious in lines of pure-bred dog.

An experienced breeder should be able to recognize a healthy puppy upon appearance; if not at birth, then certainly by the time the pup is eight weeks of age. Do not purchase a Mastiff puppy before this age. Rely upon

Bite of a five-week-old puppy. The bite will change as the pup grows. Check the bite of your chosen pup; the breeder should be able to advise you on how the bite will develop as the pup matures.

THE COCOA WARS

Chocolate contains the chemical thebromine, which is poisonous to dogs, although "chocolates" especially made for dogs are safe (as they don't actually contain chocolate) but not recommended. Any item that encourages your dog to enjoy the taste of cocoa should be discouraged. You should also exercise caution when using mulch in your yard or garden. This frequently contains cocoa hulls, and dogs have been known to die from eating mulch.

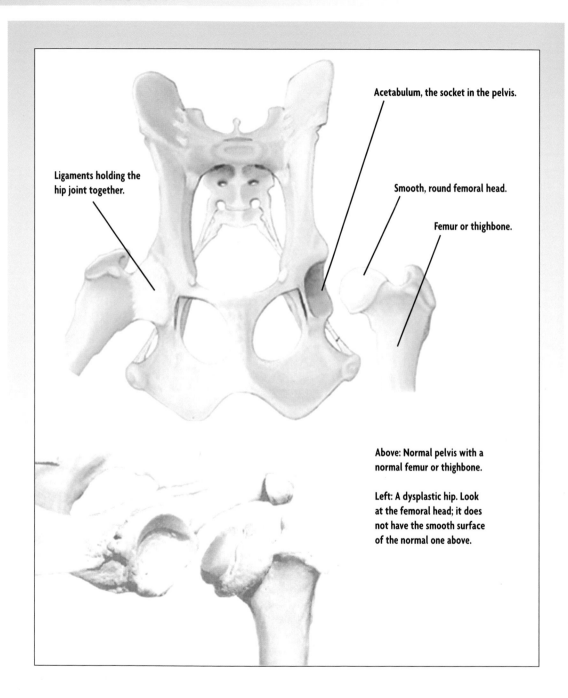

Acetabulum, the socket in the pelvis.

Ligaments holding the hip joint together.

Smooth, round femoral head.

Femur or thighbone.

Above: Normal pelvis with a normal femur or thighbone.

Left: A dysplastic hip. Look at the femoral head; it does not have the smooth surface of the normal one above.

PEDIGREE VS. REGISTRATION CERTIFICATE

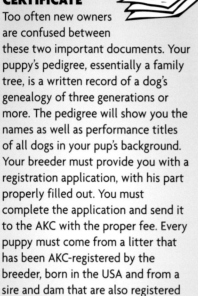

Too often new owners are confused between these two important documents. Your puppy's pedigree, essentially a family tree, is a written record of a dog's genealogy of three generations or more. The pedigree will show you the names as well as performance titles of all dogs in your pup's background. Your breeder must provide you with a registration application, with his part properly filled out. You must complete the application and send it to the AKC with the proper fee. Every puppy must come from a litter that has been AKC-registered by the breeder, born in the USA and from a sire and dam that are also registered with the AKC.

The seller must provide you with complete records to identify the puppy. The AKC requires that the seller provide the buyer with the following: breed; sex, color and markings; date of birth; litter number (when available); names and registration numbers of the parents; breeder's name; and date sold or delivered.

your breeder to determine which pup in the litter is best suited for you. Regardless of conformation, a puppy must be sound and healthy, whether entering a life as a show dog, breeding dog or companion.

The healthy puppy will be a happy, inquisitive dog with a positive attitude. He will try to get the attention of all people around him. He will even be a little selfish and seek out the attention of visitors. He will play with everything and will look lively and amicable, responding to the owner's calls without hesitation. He will look nice and clean, even if he wanders around the yard and gets into mischief. His hair will look shiny and soft, with a clean smell. The pup's rear end will be clean. The inside of his ears will look soft and pink, without any sign of irritation, and his eyes will be free of debris or discharge. The cornea will be perfectly white, the crystalline will be transparent and the conjunctiva will be

If a puppy fails to nurse from his dam, the breeder will have to bottle-feed him until he is weaned to solid foods.

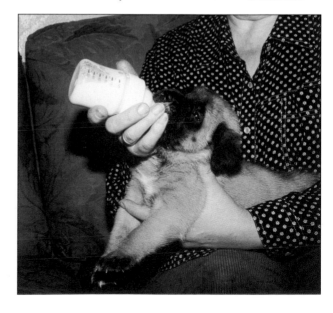

TIME TO GO HOME

Breeders rarely release puppies until they are eight to ten weeks of age. This is an acceptable age for most breeds of dog, excepting Toy breeds, which are not released until around 12 weeks, given their petite sizes. If a breeder has a puppy that is 12 weeks of age or older, he is likely well socialized and house-trained. Be sure that he is otherwise healthy before deciding to take him home.

rosy but never red. Eyelids will not be too separated from the ocular globe, the lachrymal (tear) duct will not be protruding and the eyelashes will be dry and well separated.

You must also consider the puppy's gait. His movements will be easy and relaxed, even agile. When running, his legs should not cross underneath him nor should his rear legs be dragging or limping. This is a puppy, not a rabbit. A rabbit pace is always the first sign of problems in the hindquarters, and possibly of hip dysplasia, so beware!

The Mastiff pup should be thin enough so that one can see his muscles, especially on the chest, shoulders and thighs. Fat is one of the worst enemies of big molossers. A pendulous, excessive belly—unless the puppy has just eaten—may indicate worms or other internal parasites.

From the frontal view, the chest should be wide, deep and well let down between the forequarters; the forelegs should be strong and set wide apart. Feet should be small and close. Toes should be slightly arched, neither turning in or out. In profile, the dog will be well proportioned and rectangular shaped. Fore and hind angulation should be moderate, the loins should be wide and muscular (slightly arched in dogs) and the back should be quite straight. The tail should be set on high. It should always be wider at the base, narrowing towards the tip, and should be long enough to reach the hocks. The tail should be free from deviations that could suggest a broken tail. A good way to determine this is to press softly on the coccygeal vertebrae (tail bones) with your fingers and make sure that there are no major defects in the tail. Viewing from behind, the hindquarters should also look well set apart. It will be easy to distinguish dogs from bitches from their substance and their behavior.

The head should be evaluated separately, since this is undoubtedly the breed's most unique feature. We insist on not looking for "the biggest head in the litter" when selecting a puppy. A typical Mastiff has to be much more than a giant head, but, needless to say, a young puppy with a spectacular head will also have a spectacular head in adulthood. Nevertheless, to assess the head at an early age, there is more to consider than its size. All of its parts should be proportioned. The ears should be big, their tips surpassing the upper jawbone; it is even better if they reach the lower one. According to the AKC standard, ears should be "set widely apart at highest points on the sides of the skull, continuing the outline across the summit."

Ears should also be well set apart, allowing the occipital protuberance to show in between them. The wrinkle should not be excessive. The ideal should be a crease over the frontal arch and another one, very discreet, over the eyehole. More wrinkles would be excessive in adulthood and could be associated with specific eye problems.

ARE YOU PREPARED?

Unfortunately, when a puppy is bought by someone who does not take into consideration the time and attention that dog ownership requires, it is the puppy who suffers when he is either abandoned or placed in a shelter by a frustrated owner. So all of the "homework" you do in preparation for your pup's arrival will benefit you both. The more informed you are, the more you will know what to expect and the better equipped you will be to handle the ups and downs of raising a puppy. Hopefully, everyone in the household is willing to do his part in raising and caring for the pup. The anticipation of owning a dog often brings a lot of promises from excited family members: "I will walk him every day," "I will feed him," "I will house-train him," etc., but these things take time and effort, and promises can easily be forgotten once the novelty of the new pet has worn off.

The muzzle is another important detail to consider. It should be wide from the stop to the front of the mouth. The lips should not be excessively pendulous. The bite should be preferably a scissor bite. Any frontal or lateral deviation will imply prognatism or "wry mouth" (twisted mouth) in adulthood. However, it is worth clarifying that an eight- or ten-week-old puppy can show signs of a relative superior prognatism (overbite). This should not be a concern. On the contrary, it usually guarantees that the dog will have a perfectly correct bite in adulthood. Why? Simply because the skull will go through significant modifications and adjustments in the coming months until it is fully developed. What should be worrying is if the puppy has an exaggerated lower prognatism (underbite). This could worsen with time and maturity.

Now let us consider some of the "cosmetic" traits of the puppy: color and pigmentation. One of the most attractive qualities of the Mastiff is his black mask. The ears are also darker than the coat, just like the eyes, which should be hazel brown, the darker the better. At the age of eight weeks, all of these details should be evident in the puppy. The pup's eyes cannot be light blue, green or gray, since this means that they will be yellow in adulthood. The presence of black hairs along the rims of the inside ears is a good way of determining if the ears actually will be darker than the rest of the coat when the pup reaches maturity. Light,

YOUR SCHEDULE . . .

If you lead an erratic, unpredictable life, with daily or weekly changes in your work requirements, consider the problems of owning a dog. A young puppy needs much care and attention. He has to be fed regularly, socialized (loved, petted, handled, introduced to other people) and, very importantly, allowed to visit outdoors for toilet training. As the dog gets older, he can be more tolerant of deviations in his feeding and toilet relief.

reddish, undefined facial masks imply lack of pigmentation, reminiscent of the regrettable ancestry of the Dogue de Bordeaux (the red-colored French Mastiff). Even in the case of brindle dogs, the mask should be black and well defined, and the same criteria should be followed to assess ears and eyes. Again, the eyes should be dark in color, never bluish, greenish or yellowish.

Another important aspect is coat color. The standard refers to tones of fawn and apricot, and dark brindle. Gray is not acceptable. That is why we should distinguish an overly pigmented puppy (one showing an almost black solid back hairline and an almost solid black

Black masks on Mastiff puppies are most desirable, as are dark markings on the ears. This sleeping pile of puppies shows much promise.

PUPPY PERSONALITY

When a litter becomes available to you, choosing a pup out of all those adorable faces will not be an easy task! Sound temperament is of utmost importance, but each pup has its own personality and some may be better suited to you than others. A feisty, independent pup will do well in a home with older children and adults, while quiet, shy puppies will thrive in homes with minimal noise and distractions. Your breeder knows the pups best and should be able to guide you in the right direction.

spot on the chest and the inside of the limbs, which will disappear with time) from one with an unacceptable coat color.

Puppies present what we commonly call fuzz (puppy hair), which protects them from weather changes during the first months of their lives and tends to fall off after the first shedding. However, we should be able to tell the difference between this puppy trait and a woolly, silky, thin coat, usually longer than normal, which is atypical for the breed. The coat of a Mastiff should be short and skin-tight, but not too thin on the back and the neck.

Use all of the foregoing information (and the advice of the expert breeder) to help you select a typical, sound Mastiff puppy. In every litter (hopefully!), there are some exceptional individuals that the breeder commonly reserves for

Males and females alike are loving parents, as this Mastiff dad relaxes in the sun with two of his brood.

"show homes" (or that he decides to keep for his own program). Such show-quality puppies may not be available to "pet homes," and without doubt will be the most expensive pups in the litter. A breeder cannot afford to allow his best pups not to be shown, as the success of his breeding program (and his reputation) relies upon his show-ring victories.

Ideally the breeder's litter will have many puppies that exhibit typical features of the breed. This speaks well of the breeder's ability to combine different bloodlines and to develop his own personal "stamp" on the breed, a successful breeding program. In any case, what matters most is that the breeder is honest with his puppy buyers, revealing if certain puppies are reserved for other homes, etc. This honesty helps to ensure that satisfaction is achieved by both owner and seller.

INHERIT THE MIND

In order to know whether or not a puppy will fit into your lifestyle, you need to assess his personality. A good way to do this is to interact with his parents. Your pup inherits not only his appearance but also his personality and temperament from the sire and dam. If the parents are fearful or overly aggressive, these same traits may likely show up in your puppy.

A responsible breeder will ask the potential owner to consider his instructions regarding diet, vaccinations, deworming and even the house-training and exercise of the puppy. It is very likely that the breeder will provide the new owner with a dossier with complete instructions. Never doubt your breeder, as it is assuredly he who knows what his dogs require, especially during the critical developmental months. Some breeders also will recommend particular vets who have special experience in dealing with Mastiffs and their breed-specific needs.

COMMITMENT OF OWNERSHIP
After considering all of these factors, you have most likely already made some very important decisions about selecting your puppy. You have chosen the Mastiff, which means that you have decided which characteristics you want in a dog and what type of dog will best fit into your family and lifestyle. If you have selected a breeder, you have gone a step further—you have

done your research and found a responsible, conscientious person who breeds quality Mastiffs and who should be a reliable source of help as you and your puppy adjust to life together. If you have observed a litter in action, you have obtained a firsthand look at the dynamics of a puppy pack and, thus, you have learned about each pup's individual personality—perhaps you have even found one that particularly appeals to you.

Researching your breed, selecting a responsible breeder

Are you ready to give your heart (and couch) to a Mastiff?

HANDLE WITH CARE
You should be extremely careful about handling tiny puppies. Not that you might hurt them, but that the pups' mother may exhibit what is called "maternal aggression." It is a natural, instinctive reaction for the dam to protect her young against anything she interprets as predatory or possibly harmful to her pups. The sweetest, most gentle of bitches, after whelping a litter, often reacts this way, even to her owner.

Though it is diffi-
cult to predict for
certain how well
a puppy will
develop, this
youngster repre-
sents a puppy
with great show
potential.
Mastiffs do not
mature fully until
they are almost
three years old.

and observing as many pups as possible are all important steps on the way to dog ownership. It may seem like a lot of effort...and you have not even taken the pup home yet! Remember, though, you cannot be too careful when it comes to deciding on the type of dog you want and finding out about your prospective pup's background. Buying a puppy is not—or *should* not be—just a whimsical purchase. This is one instance in which you actually do get to choose your own family! You may be thinking that buying a puppy should be fun—it should not be so serious and so much work. Keep in mind that your puppy is not a cuddly stuffed toy or decorative lawn ornament; rather, he is a living creature that will become a real member of your family. You will come to realize that, while buying a puppy is a pleasurable and exciting endeavor, it is not something to be taken lightly. Relax...the fun will start when the pup comes home!

Select a puppy that appears healthy and is responsive in every way. Use your head in your decision—although it's easy to fall for each and every pup in the litter!

A HEALTHY PUP
You should not even think about buying a puppy that looks sick, undernourished, overly frightened or nervous. Sometimes a timid puppy will warm up to you after a 30-minute "let's-get-acquainted" session.

Always keep in mind that a puppy is nothing more than a baby in a furry disguise...a baby who is virtually helpless in a human world and who trusts his owner for fulfillment of his basic needs for survival. In addition to food, water and shelter, your pup needs care, protection, guidance and love. If you are not prepared to commit to this, then you are not prepared to own a dog.

"Wait a minute," you say. "How hard could this be? All of my neighbors own dogs and they seem to be doing just fine. Why should I have to worry about all of this?" Well, you should not worry about it; in fact, you will probably find that once your Mastiff pup gets used to his new home, he will fall into his place in the family quite naturally. However, it never hurts to emphasize the commitment of dog ownership. With some time and patience, it is really not too difficult to raise a curious and exuberant Mastiff pup to be a well-adjusted and well-mannered adult dog—a dog that could be your most loyal friend.

PREPARING PUPPY'S PLACE IN YOUR HOME

Researching your breed and finding a breeder are only two aspects of the "homework" you will have to do before taking your Mastiff

ARE YOU A FIT OWNER?
If the breeder from whom you are buying a puppy asks you a lot of personal questions, do not be insulted. Such a breeder wants to be sure that you will be a fit provider for his puppy.

puppy home. You will also have to prepare your home and family for the new addition. Much as you would prepare a nursery for a newborn baby, you will need to designate a place in your home

Crate training is not commonly done with Mastiffs, though a crate can be used temporarily to instill clean toileting habits. If you purchase a crate, be certain to select one that is large enough so that the puppy doesn't outgrow it overnight!

that will be the puppy's own. How you prepare your home will depend on how much freedom the dog will be allowed. Whatever you decide, you must ensure that he has a place that he can call his own.

When you bring your new puppy into your home, you are bringing him into what will become his home as well. Obviously, you did not buy a puppy with the intentions of catering to his every whim and allowing him to "rule the roost," but in order for a puppy to grow into a stable, well-adjusted dog, he has to feel comfortable in his surroundings. Remember, he is leaving the warmth and security

A baby gate can be useful to confine the Mastiff puppy to a particular area. The dog must be trained to respect the gate, or else he will soon overcome it without any effort whatsoever.

FINANCIAL RESPONSIBILITY
Grooming tools, collars, leashes, a dog bed, perhaps a crate and, of course, toys will be expenses to you when you first obtain your pup, and the cost will continue throughout your dog's lifetime. If your puppy damages or destroys your possessions (as most puppies surely will!) or something belonging to a neighbor, you can calculate additional expense. There is also flea and pest control, which every dog owner faces more than once. You must be able to handle the financial responsibility of owning a dog.

of his mother and littermates, as well as the familiarity of the only place he has ever known, so it is important to make his transition as easy as possible. By preparing a place in your home for the puppy, you are making him feel as welcome as possible in a strange new place. It should not take him long to get used to it, but the sudden shock of being transplanted is somewhat traumatic for a young pup.

Provide a limited space for your Mastiff pup, close to the family area; about 10 to 12 feet square should suffice. Be sure that the surface of the flooring is not slippery. This is a general rule for the floors in your entire house. Mastiffs are a bit clumsy, and slipping on hardwood floors, slate or tile can cause injury to the growing pup's ligaments. You should also remove any small rugs that can slide out from under the dog's feet (or reinforce the rugs with non-slip backing).

In his special area, the dog should have his bed, his toys and his food and water bowls. During house-training, you may have to provide enough space for him to relieve himself in case he has an "accident" when left alone, though he likely will not want to use it if it is close to his sleeping and eating area. Personally, I do not recommend that the puppy's resting place be a crate, although crate-training is a popular method commonly used with many other breeds. If the owner wishes to confine the puppy to a certain area, an exercise pen made for dogs (or a similar type made for children) can offer the same effect without causing the dog stress. Mastiffs tend to panic when confined in crates, and this is not good for their emotional or physical state.

Once the puppy becomes more reliable in the house, and doesn't attempt to break or eat your furniture, then you can let him have full run of the house. Again, remember to ensure that your floors are protected. You can purchase a non-slip application for your floors.

WHAT YOU SHOULD BUY

BEDDING

Your Mastiff will welcome a nice soft bed to sleep upon, as well as a good-sized blanket. First, the blanket will take the place of the leaves, twigs, etc., that the pup would use in the wild to make a den; the pup can make his own "burrow" in his bed. Although your pup is far removed from his den-making ancestors, the

PLAY'S THE THING

Teaching the puppy to play with his toys in running and fetching games is an ideal way to help the puppy develop muscle, learn motor skills and bond with you, his owner and master. He also needs to learn how to inhibit his bite reflex and never to use his teeth on people, forbidden objects and other animals in play. Whenever you play with your puppy, you make the rules. This becomes an important message to your puppy in teaching him that you are the pack leader and control everything he does in life. Once your dog accepts you as his leader, your relationship with him will be cemented for life.

denning instinct is still a part of his genetic makeup. Second, until you take your pup home, he has been sleeping amid the warmth of his mother and littermates, and while a blanket is not the same as a warm, breathing body, it still provides heat and something with which to snuggle.

TOYS

Toys are a must for dogs of all ages, especially for curious playful pups. Puppies are the "children" of the dog world, and what child does not love toys? Chew toys provide enjoyment for both dog and owner—your dog will enjoy playing with his favorite toys, while you will enjoy the fact that they distract him from chewing on your expensive shoes and leather sofa. Puppies love to chew; in fact, chewing is a physical need for pups as they are teething, and everything looks appetizing! The full range of your possessions—from old towel to Oriental carpet—are fair game in the eyes of a teething pup. Puppies are not all that discerning when it comes to finding something literally to "sink their teeth into"—everything tastes great!

Mastiff puppies are strong, aggressive chewers and only the hardest, strongest toys of appropriate size should be offered to them. Breeders advise owners to resist stuffed and squeaky toys,

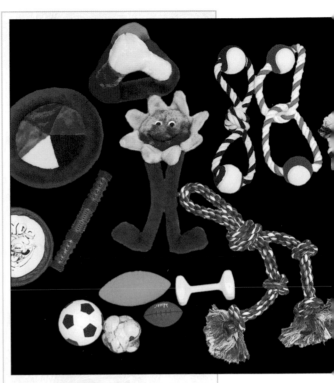

TOYS, TOYS, TOYS!

With a big variety of dog toys available, and so many that look like they would be a lot of fun for a dog, be careful in your selection. It is amazing what a set of puppy teeth can do to an innocent-looking toy, so, obviously, safety is a major consideration. Be sure to choose the most durable products that you can find. Hard nylon bones and toys are a safe bet, and many of them are offered in different scents and flavors that will be sure to capture your dog's attention. It is always fun to play a game of fetch with your dog, and there are balls and flying discs that are specially made to withstand dog teeth.

CHOOSE AN APPROPRIATE COLLAR

The **BUCKLE COLLAR** is the standard collar used for everyday purposes. Be sure that you adjust the buckle on growing puppies. Check it every day. It can become too tight overnight! These collars can be made of leather or nylon. Attach your dog's identification tags to this collar.

The **CHOKE COLLAR** is designed for training. It is constructed of highly polished steel so that it slides easily through the stainless steel loop. The idea is that the dog controls the pressure around his neck and he will stop pulling if the collar becomes uncomfortable. It should *never* be left on a dog when not training.

The **HALTER** is for a trained dog that has to be restrained to prevent running away, chasing a cat and the like. Considered the most humane of all collars, it is frequently used on smaller dogs on which collars are not comfortable.

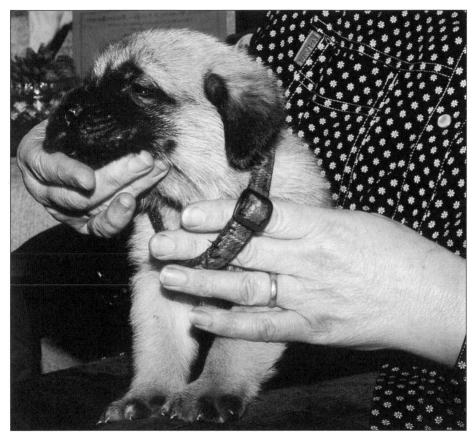

The collar for your Mastiff puppy should fit comfortably, neither too loosely nor too snugly. A persistent pup will be able to work his way out of a too-large collar.

because they can be destroyed in no time. The overly excited pup may ingest the stuffing or the "squeaker," which is neither digestible nor nutritious, or possibly swallow the toy whole!

Be careful of natural bones, which have a tendency to splinter into sharp, dangerous pieces. Also be careful of rawhide, which can turn into pieces that are easy to swallow and become a mushy mess on your carpet.

LEAD
A nylon lead is probably the best option, as it is the most resistant to puppy teeth should your pup take a liking to chewing on his lead. Of course, this is a habit that should be nipped in the bud, but, if your pup likes to chew on his lead, he has a very slim chance of being able to chew through the strong nylon. For everyday walking and safety purposes, the nylon lead is a good choice. As the

Mastiff grows up, a strong leather lead or chain lead will be your best option.

COLLAR

Your pup should get used to wearing a collar all the time since you will want to attach his ID tags to it; plus, you have to attach the lead to something! A strong nylon collar is a good choice. Make certain that the collar fits snugly enough so that the pup cannot wriggle out of it, but is loose enough so that it will not be uncomfortably tight around the pup's neck. You should be able to fit a finger between the pup's neck and the collar. It may take some time for your pup to get used to wearing the collar, but soon he will not even notice that it is there. Choke collars are made for training, but should only be used by owners who know exactly how to use them.

FOOD AND WATER BOWLS

Your pup will need two bowls, one for food and one for water. You may want two sets of bowls, one for indoors and one for outdoors, depending on where the dog will be fed and where he will be spending time. Stainless steel is the best choice for the Mastiff, as these bowls are indestructible and easily cleaned. Plastic bowls can easily be destroyed by the playful Mastiff. Invest in bowl stands to elevate your Mastiff's bowls. These stands will help

PUPPY PROBLEMS

The majority of problems that are commonly seen in young pups will disappear as your dog gets older. However, how you deal with problems when he is young will determine how he reacts to discipline as an adult dog. It is important to establish who is boss (ideally it will be you!) right away when you are first bonding with your dog. This bond will set the tone for the rest of your life together.

ward off bloat by keeping the dog from craning his neck while he eats or drinks.

CLEANING SUPPLIES

Until a pup is house-trained, you will be doing a lot of cleaning. "Accidents" will occur, which is acceptable in the beginning stages of house-training because the puppy does not know any better. All you can do is be prepared to clean up any accidents as soon as they happen. Old rags, towels, newspapers and a safe disinfectant are good to have on hand.

BEYOND THE BASICS

The items previously discussed are the bare necessities. You will find out what else you need as you go along—grooming supplies, flea/tick protection, baby gates to partition a room, etc. These things will vary depending on your situation, but it is important that you have everything you need to feed and make your Mastiff comfortable in his first few days at home.

PUPPY-PROOFING YOUR HOME

Aside from making sure that your Mastiff will be comfortable in your home, you also have to make sure that your home is safe for your Mastiff. This means taking precautions that your pup will not get into anything he should not get into and that

It is your responsibility to clean up after your dog has relieved himself. Pet shops have various aids to assist in the cleanup job.

there is nothing within his reach that may harm him should he sniff it, chew it, inspect it, etc. This probably seems obvious since, while you are primarily concerned with your pup's safety, at the same time you do not want your belongings to be ruined. Breakables should be placed out of reach if your dog is to have full run of the house. If he is to be limited to certain places within the house, keep any potentially dangerous items in the "off-limits" areas.

An electrical cord can pose a danger should the puppy decide to taste it—and who is going to convince a pup that it would not make a great chew toy? Wires and cords should be fastened tightly against the wall, out of puppy's reach. Just as you would with a child, keep all household cleaners and chemicals where the pup cannot reach them; antifreeze is particularly toxic to dogs.

It is also important to make sure that the outside of your home is safe. Of course, your puppy should never be unsuper-

FEEDING TIPS

You will probably start feeding your pup the same food that he has been getting from the breeder; the breeder should give you a few days' supply to start you off. Although you should not give your pup too many treats, you will want to have puppy treats on hand for coaxing, training, rewards, etc. Be careful, though, as a small pup's calorie requirements are relatively low and a few treats can add up to almost a full day's worth of calories without the required nutrition.

vised, but a pup let loose in the yard will want to play and explore, and he should be granted that freedom. Do not let a fence give you a false sense of security; you would be surprised at how crafty (and persistent) a dog can be in working out how to climb over or get through a fence. The remedy is to make the fence well embedded into the ground and high enough so that it really is impossible for your dog to get over it (about 6 to 7 feet should suffice). Mastiffs do not have the need to escape from the property that they are protecting, though for safety's sake, it's better to err on the side of caution. Be sure to secure any gaps in the fence. Check the fence periodically to ensure that it is in good shape and make repairs as needed.

FIRST TRIP TO THE VET

You have selected your puppy, and your home and family are ready. Now all you have to do is collect your Mastiff from the breeder and the fun begins, right? Well...not so fast. Something else you need to plan is your pup's first trip to the veterinarian. Perhaps the breeder can recommend someone in the area who specializes in large breeds, as this is critical in your choice of a vet. It is even better if you can find a vet who knows the Mastiff breed specifically.

You should have an appointment arranged for your pup before you pick him up. The pup's first visit will consist of an overall examination to make sure that the pup does not have any problems that are not apparent to you. The veterinarian will also set up program for the pup's vaccinations; the breeder will inform you of which ones the pup has already received and the vet can continue from there. I recommend that you take your pup to the vet every two weeks to check his proper growth and development.

INTRODUCTION TO THE FAMILY

Everyone in the house will be excited about the puppy's coming home and will want to pet him and play with him, but it is best to make the introductions low-key so as not to overwhelm the puppy. He is apprehensive already. It is the first time he has been separated from his mother and the breeder, and the ride to your home is likely to be the first time he has been in a car. The last thing you want to do is smother him, as this will only frighten him further. This is not to say that human contact is not extremely necessary at this stage, because this is the time when a connection between the pup and his human family is formed. Gentle petting and

NATURAL TOXINS

Examine your grass and landscaping before bringing your puppy home. Many varieties of plants have leaves, stems or flowers that are toxic if ingested, and you can depend on a curious puppy to investigate them. Ask your vet for information on poisonous plants or research them at your library.

If you see your dog carrying a piece of vegetation in his mouth, approach him in a quiet disinterested manner, avoid eye contact, pet him and gradually remove the plant from his mouth. Alternatively, offer him a treat and maybe he'll drop the plant on his own accord. Be sure no toxic plants are growing in your own yard or kept in your home.

Providing toys to your Mastiff puppy will do wonders for your shoes. If you don't provide safe chew toys, your puppy will improvise—and likely not to your liking.

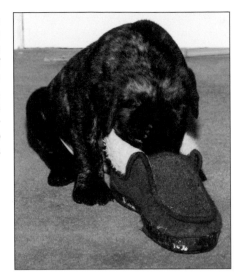

soothing words should help console him, as well as just putting him down and letting him explore on his own (under your watchful eye, of course).

The pup may approach the family members or may busy himself with exploring for a while. Gradually, each person should spend some time with the pup, one at a time, crouching down to get as close to the pup's level as possible, letting him sniff their hands and petting him gently. He definitely needs human attention and he needs to be touched—this is how to form an immediate bond. Just remember that the pup is experiencing many things for the first time, at the same time. There are new people, new noises, new smells and new things to investigate, so be gentle, be affectionate and be as comforting as you can be.

PUP'S FIRST NIGHT HOME

You have traveled home with your new charge. He's been to the vet for a thorough check-up; he's been weighed, his papers have been examined and perhaps he's even been vaccinated and wormed as well. He's met the whole family, including the excited children and the less-than-happy cat. He's explored his area, his new bed, the yard and anywhere else he's been permitted. He's eaten his first meal at home and relieved himself in the proper place. He's heard lots of new sounds, smelled new friends and seen more of the outside world than ever before...and that was just the first day! He's worn out and is ready for bed...or so you think!

It's puppy's first night home and you are ready to say "Good night." Keep in mind that this is

SKULL & CROSSBONES

Thoroughly puppy-proof your house before bringing your puppy home. Never use cockroach or rodent poisons or plant fertilizers in any area accessible to the puppy. Avoid the use of toilet cleaners. Most dogs are born with "toilet-bowl sonar" and will take a drink if the lid is left open. Also keep the trash secured and out of reach.

his first night ever to be sleeping alone. His dam and littermates are no longer at paw's length and he's a bit scared, cold and lonely. Be reassuring to your new family member, but this is not the time to spoil him and give in to his inevitable whining.

Puppies whine to let others know where they are and hopefully to get company out of it. At bedtime, place your pup in his new bed in his designated area. Mercifully, he may fall asleep without a peep. When the inevitable occurs, however, ignore the whining—he is fine. Be strong and keep his interest in mind. Do not allow yourself to feel guilty and visit the pup. He will fall asleep eventually.

Many breeders recommend placing a piece of bedding from the pup's former home in his new bed so that he recognizes and is comforted by the scent of his littermates. Others still advise placing a hot water bottle in the bed for warmth. The latter may be a good idea provided the pup doesn't attempt to suckle— he'll get good and wet, and may not fall asleep so fast.

Puppy's first night can be somewhat stressful for both the pup and his new family. Remember that you are setting the tone of nighttime at your house. Unless you want to play with your pup every night at 10 p.m., midnight and 2 a.m., don't

initiate the habit. Your family will thank you, and soon so will your pup!

SOCIALIZATION
Now that you have done all of the preparatory work and have helped your pup get accustomed to his new home and family, it is about time for you to have some fun! Socializing your Mastiff pup gives you the opportunity to show off your new friend, and your pup gets to reap the benefits of being a

STRESS-FREE
Some experts in canine health advise that stress during a dog's early years of development can compromise and weaken his immune system, and may trigger the potential for a shortened life. They emphasize the need for happy and stress-free growing-up years.

Engage your puppy in play with chew-worthy toys. A Mastiff puppy can destroy average dog toys in a matter of minutes.

fabulous molosser creature that people will want to meet and admire.

Besides getting to know his new family, your puppy should be exposed to other people, animals and situations. This will help him become well adjusted as he grows up and less prone to being timid or fearful of the new things he will encounter. Of course, he must not come into close contact with dogs you don't know well until his course of injections is fully complete.

Your pup's socialization began with the breeder, but now it is your responsibility to continue it. The socialization he receives until the age of 12 weeks is the most critical, as this is the time when he forms his impressions of the outside world. Be especially careful during the eight-to-ten-week-old period, also known as the fear period. The

PUP MEETS WORLD

Thorough socialization includes not only meeting new people but also being introduced to new experiences such as riding in the car, having his coat brushed, hearing the television, walking in a crowd—the list is endless. The more your pup experiences, and the more positive the experiences are, the less of a shock and the less frightening it will be for your pup to encounter new things.

interaction he receives during this time should be gentle and reassuring. Lack of socialization, and/or negative experiences during the socialization period, can manifest itself in fear and insecurity as the dog grows up. Your puppy needs lots of positive interaction, which of course includes human contact, affection, handling and exposure to other animals.

Once your pup has received his necessary vaccinations, feel free to take him out and about (on his lead, of course). Walk him around the neighborhood, take him on your daily errands, let people pet him, let him meet other dogs and pets, etc. Puppies do not have to try to make friends; there will be no shortage of people who will want to introduce themselves. Just make sure that you carefully supervise each meeting. What a pup learns during this very formative stage will affect his attitude toward future encounters. You want your dog to be comfortable around everyone. For example, a pup that has a bad experience with a child may grow up to be a dog that is shy around or aggressive toward children, which is a totally unacceptable scenario with any dog, especially one as powerful as the Mastiff.

COMMON PUPPY PROBLEMS

The best way to prevent puppy problems is to be proactive in

MANNERS MATTER
During the socialization process, a puppy should meet people, experience different environments and definitely be exposed to other canines. Through playing and interacting with other dogs, your puppy will learn lessons, ranging from controlling the pressure of his jaws by biting his littermates to the inner-workings of the canine pack that he will apply to his human relationships for the rest of his life. That is why removing a puppy from the litter too early (before eight weeks) can be detrimental to the pup's development.

stopping an undesirable behavior as soon as it starts. The old saying "You can't teach an old dog new tricks" does not necessarily hold true, but it *is* true that it is much easier to discourage bad behavior in a young developing pup than to wait until the pup's bad behavior becomes the adult dog's bad habit. There are some problems that are especially prevalent in puppies as they develop.

NIPPING
As puppies start to teethe, they feel the need to sink their teeth into anything available...unfortunately, that usually includes your fingers, arms, hair and toes. You

Once dogs are socialized with each other, they usually become true friends as this Mastiff and Bulldog demonstrate.

may find this behavior cute for the first five seconds...until you feel just how sharp those puppy teeth are. Nipping is something you want to discourage immediately and consistently with a firm "No!" (or whatever number of firm "Nos" it takes for him to understand that you mean business). Then, replace your finger with an appropriate chew toy. While this behavior is merely annoying when the dog is young, it can become

PROPER SOCIALIZATION

The socialization period for puppies is from age 8 to 16 weeks. This is the time when puppies need to leave their birth family and take up residence with their new owners, where they will meet many new people, other pets, etc. Failure to be adequately socialized can cause the dog to grow up fearing others and being shy and unfriendly due to a lack of self-confidence.

dangerous as your Mastiff's adult teeth grow in and his jaws develop if he thinks that it is okay to nibble on his human friends. Your Mastiff pup does not mean any harm with a friendly nip, but he also does not know his own strength, which grows more and more amazing with every passing day.

CRYING/WHINING

We know that Mastiffs desire nothing as much as human contact and friendship. Your pup

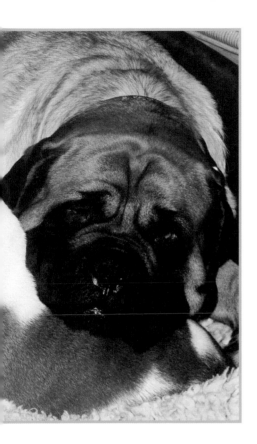

he needs to be taught that being alone is okay. You do not actually train the dog to stop making noise; rather, you acclimate him to his area and teach him to feel comfortable when he is alone, thus removing the need for him to make the noise.

CHEWING TIPS

Chewing goes hand in hand with nipping in the sense that a teething puppy is always looking for a way to soothe his aching gums. In this case, instead of chewing on you, he may have taken a liking to your favorite shoe or something else that he should not be chewing. Again, realize that this is a normal canine behavior that does not need to be discouraged, only redirected. Your pup just needs to be taught what is acceptable to chew on and what is off-limits. Consistently tell him "No!" when you catch him chewing on something forbidden and give him a chew toy.

Conversely, praise him when you catch him chewing on something appropriate. In this way, you are discouraging the inappropriate behavior and reinforcing the desired behavior. The puppy's chewing should stop after his adult teeth have come in, but an adult dog continues to chew for various reasons—perhaps because he is bored, needs to relieve tension or just likes to chew. That is why it is important to redirect his chewing when he is still young.

will often cry, whine, whimper, howl or make some type of commotion when he is left alone. This is basically his way of calling out for attention to make sure that you know he is there and that you have not forgotten about him. Your puppy feels insecure when he is left alone, when you are out of the house and he is in his special area or when you are in another part of the house and he cannot see you. The noise he is making is an expression of the anxiety he feels at being alone, so

FEEDING THE MASTIFF

Since there are so many types of dog food on the market, the choices of formulations and brands are overwhelming. For the Mastiff, feeding is not as simple as with many other breeds that do not undergo such dramatic weight gains and growth spurts. Additionally, studies have indicated that many of the problems directly related to bone malformations are the results of incorrect feeding or overuse of certain mineral supplements, such as calcium, during the dog's critical growth stage. Several experts even sustain that some allergies and hypothyroidism are also related to nutrition deficiency, which also weakens the dog's immune system.

Others purport that commercial food is likely linked to certain types of cancer as well as behavioral problems such as excessive shyness and aggression. It is the content of the foods, due to the excess of additives, preservatives, flavorings, antioxidants and other chemicals, that is allegedly at fault.

I do not intend to incite a riot or a protest against the large dog-food manufacturers. Instead, my approach to feeding Mastiffs, which I have used for many years now with all of my dogs

STORING DOG FOOD

You must store your dry dog food carefully. Open packages of dog food quickly lose their vitamin value, usually within 90 days of being opened. Mold spores and vermin could also contaminate the food.

with considerable success, involves offering fresh products (fruits, vegetables, meat and fish), along with an optimum-quality commercial food. During all of the years that I've practiced this method, I have seen how my dogs have improved in their quality of life, their appearance and their health, enjoying freedom from the aforementioned problems related to solely commercial feeding.

Another most important consideration when feeding the Mastiff puppy is preventing the dog from growing any faster than Nature intends. To that aim, it is best to make sure that he is fed appropriately to his needs. A giant-breed puppy should neither grow too fast nor stop growing too soon. Mastiff pups do not need too much protein, so a dry food that contains 25–28% protein is ideal, not those formulas with up to or over 33% protein. What the puppy really needs is quality protein and a perfectly balanced diet.

TEST FOR PROPER DIET
A good test for proper diet is the color, odor and firmness of your dog's stool. A healthy dog usually produces three semi-hard stools per day. The stools should have no unpleasant odor. They should be the same color from excretion to excretion.

THE MASTIFF PUPPY'S DIET
I personally recommend the following diet for the growing Mastiff pup.

From two to five months (four daily feedings):

At breakfast (B): 1.5 cups of quality prepared food (adult maintenance), softened in warm water for ten minutes, mixed with a scrambled egg and half a cup of goat's milk. Three times a week, the egg should be substituted for natural skimmed yogurt.

At lunchtime (L): About 9 ounces of raw, minced beef meat or yearling (suitable for human consumption), chicken, lamb or even heart, liver or stomach. Two or three times a week, the meat should be substituted for fresh blue fish (without bones or scales, but with its skin).

In the afternoon (A): Two raw apples quartered, with the skin, or any other fresh fruit of the season (e.g., two ripe peeled bananas,

The Mastiff puppy requires special dietary considerations. Discuss these with your breeder and vet or follow the guidelines presented here.

two peeled oranges or sweet mandarins, a very ripe peeled avocado or a big bunch of grapes).

At supper (S): 1.5 cups of quality prepared food (adult maintenance), softened in warm water for 10 minutes, mixed with about 7 to 9 ounces of fresh vegetables (carrots, asparagus, broccoli, cabbage, cauliflower, celery, squash, turnip, etc). Vegetables should be rinsed thoroughly and then put in a food processor or blender until the pieces are very small—about the size of the head of a pin—and later mixed with the rest of the food. They should always be given uncooked and unpeeled so that they do not lose their vitamin content. The reason for blending the vegetables first is that all other carnivores' intestines are much smaller in size and length than those of humans; therefore, during the digestive process, vegetables in large pieces do not have the time necessary to be broken down efficiently. Large pieces will therefore go undigested, without the full vitamin and mineral content's being absorbed into the body, thus causing nutrient deficiency in the animal.

Fresh fruits (mainly apples with the skin, pears, oranges, mandarins, bananas and avocados) should also be fed daily; yet, because fruit is digested much more quickly than dry food and

vegetables, it should be fed by itself, either during the day or at least half an hour before or after the main meals.

From five months on (three daily feedings):

At breakfast: 2–3 cups of quality prepared food (adult maintenance), dry, mixed with (L) from the previous section. Once or twice a week, a scrambled egg will be added.

In the afternoon: Same as (A) from the previous section.

At supper: 2–3 cups of quality prepared food (adult maintenance), dry, mixed with vegetables as indicated in (S) from the previous section.

THE ADULT MASTIFF'S DIET
Ideally, after the age of one year, Mastiffs should continue to eat three times per day. Nevertheless, due to some owners' schedules, this may not be possible. In such cases, it is acceptable for the Mastiff to be fed twice a day. The morning meal should be one-third of the total daily intake and the evening meal should be fed right before going to bed.

I would suggest that the adult diet remain similar to that described for the growing puppy, although the quantities of course should be adjusted to each individual dog's activity level, sex, age and size. Your vet and breeder will gladly provide you with all of the information needed to adapt the diet to each dog's lifestyle and needs.

ADDITIONAL TIPS

I know from experience that each animal must have his own bowls for eating and drinking. The bowl should always be placed at elbow level to avoid the Mastiff's swallowing too much air while eating. You can purchase bowl stands at your local pet shop, where you buy those indestructible stainless steel bowls. By doing this, you will prevent what is actually one of the biggest daily risks for the Mastiff: bloat.

Your Mastiff should always have fresh water available and it is essential to wash his drinking bowl twice a day so that any saliva is removed. Saliva can alter the taste of the water to the point that your Mastiff stops enjoying his water. If the Mastiff spends time in the yard, he should have an additional drinking bowl outside, which should be placed away from the sun, dirt and fallen leaves. This bowl also should be cleaned twice a day at the minimum.

BLOAT

Bloat is a serious condition directly related to feeding, so deserves mention here. All dogs that weigh over 75 lb and/or those with deep chests tend to suffer at one time or another from what is

WEANING PUPPIES

Puppies instinctively want to suck milk from their mother's teats; a normal puppy will exhibit this behavior just a few moments following birth. If puppies do not attempt to suckle within the first half-hour or so, the breeder should encourage them to do so by placing them on the nipples, having selected ones with plenty of milk. This early milk supply is important in providing the essential colostrum, which protects the puppies during the first eight to ten weeks of their lives. Although a mother's milk is much better than any milk formula, despite there being some excellent ones available, if the puppies do not feed, the breeder will have to feed them by hand. Puppies should be allowed to nurse from their mothers for about the first six weeks, although, starting around the third or fourth week, the breeder will begin to introduce small portions of suitable solid food. Most breeders like to introduce alternate milk and meat meals initially, building up to weaning time.

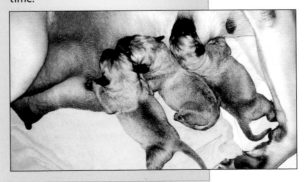

TRY TO PREVENT BLOAT
- Do not exercise your Mastiff immediately before feeding (there should be at least an hour in between);
- Do not exercise your Mastiff immediately after feeding (wait at least two to three hours);
- Do not feed cheap, high-cereal-content food;
- Feed a low-residue diet;
- Ensure that excessive quantities of water are not drunk right before or after a meal; if necessary, restrict water intake at those times;
- Elevate food and water bowls to try to reduce any air swallowed;
- If your Mastiff is greedy and eats quickly, reduce the air swallowed by putting something large and inedible in the bowl (one or two tennis balls work well with the Mastiff) so that the dog has to pick around it and thus eat more slowly.

known as volvulus or gastric dilatation, which is colloquially called "bloat." Causes of the condition are not yet clear, though several studies are underway to determine them. However, breeders, vets and experienced owners seem to agree that the main risk factors could be the following:

- Continuous ingestion of large quantities of dry food, with or without drinking plenty of water to digest it, or fast ingestion without proper chewing. This can cause the food's fermentation in the stomach, allowing the excessive production of gas.
- Vigorous exercise (running, jumping, going up and down the stairs, playing with other dogs, etc.) within an hour before or two to three hours after eating.
- Stress, manifested in the dog's excessive panting and salivation.
- Gestation of a litter with a large number of fetuses (more than six), especially during the last two weeks. During the final weeks of gestation, it is essential for breeders to divide the bitch's feedings into four or six smaller meals.
- Heredity.

Bloat is a relatively frequent and highly risky condition that can cause death if it is not identified, diagnosed and treated on time. Since the survival rate is low, it is advisable to take every possible precaution to avoid its onset.

Symptoms of bloat are almost always easy to recognize. The dog looks nervous, feels nauseous and tries unsuccessfully to vomit or drools a very dense saliva (without passing any of his stomach's contents). Almost immediately after that, his stomach swells enormously, making him more nervous. He tries to sit or lie down, but he can't, and, when he tries, he immediately gets up, visi-

(Left) Cross section through a Mastiff, showing how deep the body cavity is. The muscles around the vertebrae give strength to the back.

(Right) The stomach hangs like a handbag with both straps broken within this deep body cavity. Support is provided by the junction with the esophagus and the junction with the duodenum.

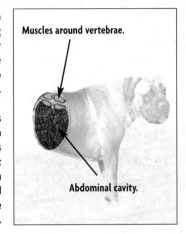

Muscles around vertebrae.

Abdominal cavity.

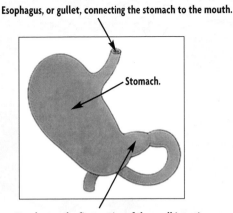

Esophagus, or gullet, connecting the stomach to the mouth.

Stomach.

Duodenum, the first section of the small intestine.

bly in pain. He might or might not complain with very specific sounds, as if he was trying to clear his throat. This is a real emergency and not a second should be wasted in getting to the veterinarian. The Mastiff's life depends on your immediate action, as he can go into shock at any moment.

What exactly is bloat? The first thing we have to understand is that the stomach of a dog is supported by two rather weak ligaments, located one at each end of the stomach sac. During the

Aside from the support provided by the junction with the esophagus, or gullet, and the support provided by the junction with the first part of the small intestine, the "broken straps of the hand-bag," the only other support is from a thin layer of partially opaque "internal skin" called the peritoneum. No wonder the stomach can move around easily, and those breeds with the deepest chests are at the greatest risk.

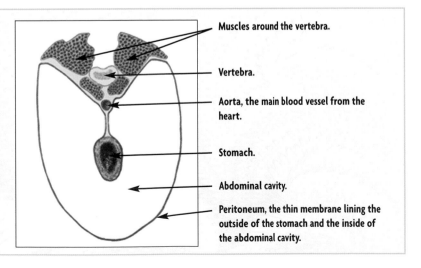

Muscles around the vertebra.

Vertebra.

Aorta, the main blood vessel from the heart.

Stomach.

Abdominal cavity.

Peritoneum, the thin membrane lining the outside of the stomach and the inside of the abdominal cavity.

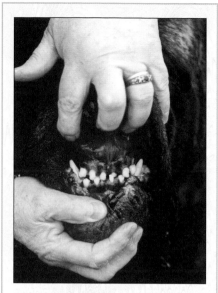

DEADLY DECAY
Did you know that periodontal disease
(a condition of the bone and gums
surrounding a tooth) can be fatal?
Having your dog's teeth and mouth
checked yearly, along with a proper
diet and dental care at home, can
prevent it.

digestion process, which can last
a few hours, gases are released
outside the body in the form of
belching or flatulence. However,
when food fermentation takes
place (especially of dry food), it
produces an accumulation of
gases in the stomach, which
cannot be released at the appropriate speed. The dog, in an effort
to relieve himself, drinks plenty
of water. Thus, stress, excessive
salivation and vigorous exercise

after eating can lead to the problem of volvulus.

Let us not forget that the
Mastiff is a deep-chested animal
of tremendous proportions. When
the stomach sac is filled with gas,
it can distend so much as to
double its size in a matter of
minutes. It can thus twist partially
or totally very easily.

The consequences are fatal
since, besides interrupting digestion, it interrupts blood circulation in both directions, leading
to shock. Even if the dog receives
medical attention in time, other
negative effects can appear in the
long run. It is also possible for a
dog to have more than one inci-
dent of bloat, even if he has had
his stomach stapled, a procedure
in which the stomach is stapled
to the inside of the chest wall to
provide extra support and
prevent its twisting again.
Therefore, there is no excuse for
not keeping up with all of the
preventative measures, even if
the dog has been operated on. It
is *always* better to prevent rather
than to treat bloat.

EXERCISE FOR THE MASTIFF
Before we discuss the needed
activity for a Mastiff, let's first
talk about rest! The importance
of rest for a growing puppy has
not been emphasized sufficiently
in past years. Just as pediatri-
cians confirm that our human
babies need 18 hours of sleep per

day, so too do our growing puppies need plenty of sleep. A puppy's life essentially consists of eating, sleeping, relieving himself, learning a bit about something or other, then sleeping again—and then repeating the routine.

Having said that, let's now discuss exercise. This giant breed does not need much exercise. It has been widely asserted that excessive exercise before the first 18 months of a Mastiff's life is very harmful. Such a regimen, combined with an inadequate diet, contributes to serious bone problems in the dog. You essentially should not take your young Mastiff for walks that last more than five to ten minutes each. More than ten minutes on a walk (two or three times a day) will not show any ill effects on the puppy right away; however, in two or three months, these walks will show up in the form of bills coming from your frustrated veterinarian, who will not be able to do anything after you have injured your pup's bones and ligaments by trotting about the neighborhood all morning.

While in the yard, your Mastiff puppy should remain under supervision. You should not expose your pup to unsupervised play sessions with other dogs, nor should play sessions last for long periods of time, as these may also stress the pup's

frame. It is also essential to limit the pup's time spent playing with children. Children and pups have a fantastic time together, but it is extremely tiring for the pup. Do not let your pup have long play periods with a child or the exhaustion will have an ill effect on the pup.

The one exercise that the author recommends, provided the weather is temperate, is supervised swimming. This is the healthiest, most natural way of developing muscles on a

Everyday bloat precautions such as elevating food and water bowls and restricting exercise require little effort on your part, but can save your Mastiff's life.

young animal. It is also the only exercise that does not pose a threat of stressing his muscular and skeletal systems. If possible, the ideal should be a 10- to 30-minute swim each day in a swimming pool, pond, bay or other safe body of water. Of course, the owner must be cognizant of the risks of swimming in streams as well as the possibilities of contamination by pollutants. After a swim, the puppy will need a good drying to prevent problems related to arthritis and rheumatism.

The owner can relax the exercise rules a bit once the pup is 18 months old. At this point, once the dog's critical growth has been accomplished, the owner can introduce the dog to more intensive exercise, possibly including agility or other trials. Many Mastiffs participate in agility competition, as well as carting, search and rescue, obedience events and weight-pulling contests.

GROOMING

COAT MAINTENANCE

Grooming the Mastiff is mostly a simple chore. This is a short-haired dog that requires two or three weekly brushings. First, brush against the grain, then with the grain to eliminate dead hairs and debris. Brushing should be done using a rubber-toothed hound glove to keep the Mastiff

perfectly clean. Contrary to what many people think, bathing is completely discouraged for this breed. Usually, dogs that are frequently bathed by their owners (let us say three or four times a year or more) end up suffering from skin problems (moist dermatitis or hot spots), which are very difficult to eradicate.

Fawn-colored Mastiffs, which have denser undercoats, tend to lose more hair than the brindle-colored dogs, which hardly lose any hair. Usually, under normal weather conditions, their shedding season takes place once a year, but if the dogs are brushed regularly, the shedding won't even be noticed.

TEETH, EARS, ANAL SACS AND NAILS

Teeth do not usually present a problem in the Mastiff. Brushing the teeth is advised by many vets, but the author has found that feeding apples with the skin on is also excellent for the dog's teeth, just as it is magnificent for overall health.

BANDOG BAN
Never tie a dog out to a post or tree, thinking that you are giving him exercise. This will only serve to increase aggression in the dog; with a breed that is naturally protective, tying the dog out can make the him mean.

Ears could present a few problems, especially if the dog gets used to spending long hours in the yard or if he lives in a particularly dusty area. Check the ears on a weekly basis to ensure that they are pink and clean on the inside, without any sign of irritation. It is also beneficial to go over the ears with a soft wipe and a cleaning solution or a little olive oil. Only wipe the areas where you can reach with your finger, the crease inside the external and the medium ear. This can be done on a monthly basis to remove any wax that accumulates. Never probe into the dog's ear, as this can cause harm. If you cannot clean your Mastiff's ears properly, be sure to ask the vet to handle it for you.

Likewise, you should check the dog's anal glands monthly, especially in males. Have your vet show you how to check them and how to express them if they become filled. The sacs can become impacted and cause the dog discomfort. However, if you do not feel comfortable with expressing the sacs yourself, take your dog to the vet every four to six weeks for that purpose.

It is essential to keep your Mastiff's nails short. Some dogs will naturally wear them down, depending on the surfaces on which they walk. Most, however, will require having their nails

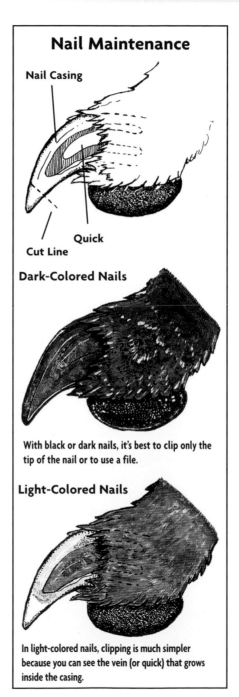

Nail Maintenance

Nail Casing

Quick

Cut Line

Dark-Colored Nails

With black or dark nails, it's best to clip only the tip of the nail or to use a file.

Light-Colored Nails

In light-colored nails, clipping is much simpler because you can see the vein (or quick) that grows inside the casing.

Clean the outer part of the ear with a soft cloth. Never probe into the ear canal.

Use a rubber-toothed hound glove, or similar device, to groom your Mastiff. Routine brushing will keep his coat glistening and remove dead hairs.

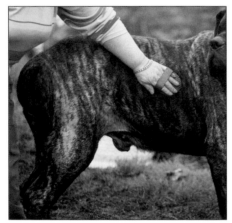

Do not neglect the care of your Mastiff's teeth and mouth. Wipe the teeth and gum areas before you begin brushing.

cut frequently. It is important to accustom the puppy to this procedure, which should be done every 10 to 12 days before the nails grow too long. Long nails hinder the dog's ability to support himself and can become ingrown and infected. If the owner cannot clip the nails himself, it is worth an extra trip to the vet. Overgrown nails can be painful to the dog and cause splayed feet.

Before you start cutting, make sure you can identify the "quick" in each nail. The quick is a blood vessel that runs through the center of each nail and grows rather close to the end. The quick will bleed if accidentally cut, which will be quite painful for the dog as it contains nerve endings. Keep some type of clotting agent on hand, such as a styptic pencil or styptic powder (the type used for shaving). This will stop the bleeding quickly when applied to the end of the cut nail. Do not panic if you cut the quick, just stop the bleeding and talk soothingly to your dog. Once he has calmed down, move on to the next nail. It is better to clip a little at a time, particularly with dark-nailed dogs.

Hold your pup steady as you begin trimming his nails; you do not want him to make any sudden movements or run away. Talk to him soothingly and stroke him as you clip. Holding his foot in your hand, simply take off the end of each nail with one swift clip. You should purchase heavy-duty guillotine-type nail clippers that are made for use on dogs; you can probably find them wherever you buy pet supplies.

TRAVEL CONSIDERATIONS

CAR TRAVEL

You should accustom your Mastiff to riding in your vehicle at an early age. You may or may not take him out and about often, but at the very least he will need to go to the vet and you do not want these trips to be traumatic for the dog or troublesome for you. For a young pup, you may opt to use a safety harness, which straps the dog in much like a seat belt. Do not let the dog roam loose in the vehicle—this is very dangerous! If you should stop short, your dog can be thrown and injured. If the dog starts climbing on you and pestering you while you are driving, you will not be able to concentrate on the road.

One of the requirements of owning a Mastiff is driving a Mastiff-sized vehicle. A sport-utility vehicle or van will be necessary to transport your dog. You can use a partition to section off a secure area in the vehicle in which your dog can travel safely, or you can purchase an appropri-

ately-sized travel crate. Since emergencies can occur with the Mastiff, it's vital to be able to haul your enormous chum to the vet's office whenever necessary.

VACATIONS AND BOARDING

So you want to take a family vacation—and you want to include *all* members of the family. You would probably make arrangements for accommodations ahead of time anyway, but this is especially

If your car can't accommodate a Mastiff-sized travel crate, you'll have to explore other options for safe travel. The rear section of a station wagon, when secured with a suitable partition, can serve to safely confine your Mastiff during car rides.

TRAVEL ALERT

Never leave your dog alone in the car. In hot weather, your dog can die from the high temperature inside a closed vehicle; even a car parked in the shade can heat up very quickly. Leaving the window open is dangerous as well since the dog can hurt himself trying to get out.

important when traveling with a dog...even more so with a dog the size of the Mastiff. You do not want to make an overnight stop at the only place around for miles, only to find out that they do not allow dogs or that they have size restrictions on the dogs that they allow. Also, you do not want to reserve a place for your family without confirming that you are traveling with a dog—a *big* dog—because, if it is against the hotel's policy, you may end up without a place to stay.

Alternatively, if you are traveling and choose not to bring your Mastiff, you will have to make arrangements for him while you are away. Some options are to have a trusted friend stay with the dog in your home or to solicit the service of a kennel. If you choose to board him at a kennel, you should visit in advance to see the facilities provided and where the dogs are kept. Are the dogs' areas spacious and kept clean? Talk to some of the employees and observe how they treat the dogs—

do they spend time with the dogs, play with them, exercise them, etc.? Are they accustomed to handling a dog as large as the Mastiff, or will they be skittish with your friend? Also find out the kennel's policy on vaccinations and what they require. This is for all of the dogs' safety, since there is a greater risk of diseases being passed from dog to dog when dogs are kept together.

You also should consider whether your Mastiff will accept strangers taking care of him at the kennel. In a strange environment, your Mastiff may not eat and be well. Most Mastiff owners concur that every day at home with a Mastiff is a vacation!

IDENTIFICATION
Your Mastiff is your valued companion and friend. That is why you always keep a close eye on him and you have made sure that he cannot escape from the yard or slip out of his collar and get lost. However, accidents can happen and there may come a time when your dog unexpectedly becomes separated from you. If this unfortunate event should occur, the first thing on your mind will be finding him. Proper identification, including an ID tag and possibly a tattoo or a microchip, will increase the chances of his being returned to you safely and quickly.

TRAINING YOUR

MASTIFF

Living with an untrained dog is not wise and certainly not pleasant, especially when you're dealing with a giant breed like the Mastiff. Any dog is a big responsibility and, if not training sensibly, may develop unacceptable behavior that annoys you or could even cause family friction or problems with your neighbors.

Mastiffs are always looking for the approval and affection of their family members, and all they need is a word of praise, kindly whispered, to feel encouraged to continue behaving properly.

The Mastiff is an extremely intelligent breed, yet they will not do things in a conventional way. Therefore, their training and instruction needs to be somewhat different than that of other canines. Because the breed is so intelligent, if you let your Mastiff do things his own way without any training or education, you could very well end up being manipulated and maneuvered by this gentle giant in such a way that he will become your master, not the other way around.

Many who have never owned a Mastiff, or who have had the

opportunity to meet one but not really bond with him, will say that the breed cannot be trained to

REAP THE REWARDS

If you start with a normal, healthy dog and give him time, patience and some carefully executed lessons, you will reap the rewards of that training for the life of the dog. And what a life it will be! The two of you will find immeasurable pleasure in the companionship you have built together with love, respect and understanding.

basic obedience or anything of the sort. Yet Mastiffs perform in many capacities—from starring in movies to working as therapy and search-and-rescue dogs; others participate successfully in tracking, carting, agility and the highest levels of obedience. Therefore, it can be said that Mastiffs are indeed quite trainable—in their own way.

What Mastiffs need most is to be treated in a gentle manner, as they can become upset easily by shouting, harsh corrections and harsh punishment. They do, however, react rather well to more modern training methods that focus on motivation and positive reinforcement to encourage the dog to do something. Using food and play during their training sessions will help Mastiffs feel quite enthusiastic about being taught to do something.

Training sessions for the Mastiff need to be short and enjoyable, and should begin as early as eight weeks of age; this is the best time to start the Mastiff with commands like sit, come, down and stay. An excellent choice is for you and the puppy to join one of the "kindergarten" classes, which are becoming more and more easy to find, once the pup is fully vaccinated—that is, from four to six months of age. These puppy classes are great fun and a wonderful means of offering socialization not only with other

PARENTAL GUIDANCE
Training a dog is a life experience. Many parents admit that much of what they know about raising children they learned from caring for their dogs. Dogs respond to love, fairness and guidance, just as children do. Become a good dog owner and you may become an even better parent.

canines but also with strangers, while at the same time teaching the pups the same basic commands that you've already started at home (sit, come, etc.). In the class, though, the pup practices the commands among distractions and interactions with strangers.

After six months of age, you may like to enroll in an obedience class. Teach your young dog good manners as you learn how and why he behaves the way he does. Find out how to communicate with your dog and how to recognize and understand his communications with you. Suddenly the dog takes on a new role in your life—he is clever, interesting, well behaved and fun to be with. He demonstrates his bond of devotion to you daily. In other words, your Mastiff does wonders for your ego because he constantly reminds you that you are not only his leader, you are his hero!

Those involved with teaching dog obedience and counseling owners about their dogs' behavior have discovered some interesting facts about dog ownership. For example, training dogs when they are puppies results in the highest rate of success in developing well-mannered and well-adjusted adult dogs. Training an adult dog can produce almost equal results, providing that the owner accepts the dog's slower rate of learning capability and is willing to work patiently to help the dog succeed at developing to his fullest potential. Unfortunately, many owners of untrained adult dogs lack the patience factor, so they do not persist until their dogs are successful at learning particular behaviors.

You must keep in mind, from the very start, that training a puppy from early puppyhood (i.e., eight weeks of age onward to one year of age, because Mastiffs are "puppies" for much longer than other breeds) is like working with a dry sponge in a pool of water. The pup soaks up whatever you show him and constantly looks for more things to do and learn.

As mentioned previously, you usually will be able to find obedience classes within a reasonable distance from your home, but you also can choose just to train your dog yourself, especially if you already have first-hand experience with molosser breeds. It is a fact

that no dog, whether puppy or adult, likes harsh or inhumane methods. All creatures, however, respond favorably to gentle motivational methods and sincere praise and encouragement.

HOUSE-TRAINING

You can train a puppy to relieve himself wherever you choose, but this must be somewhere suitable. You should bear in mind from the outset that when your

Your young Mastiff is a giant sponge waiting to soak up everything you teach him. Begin training early so that your pup's education begins before his hormones claim control of his brain.

puppy is old enough to go out in public places, any canine deposits must be removed at once. You will always have to carry with you a plastic bag or "poop-scoop."

Outdoor training includes such surfaces as grass, soil and cement. Indoor training usually means training your dog to newspaper, which is not a viable option with a dog the size of the Mastiff. When deciding on the surface and location that you will want your Mastiff to use, be sure it is going to be permanent. Training your dog to grass and then changing your mind a few months later is extremely difficult for both dog and owner.

Next, choose the command you will use each and every time you want your puppy to void. "Hurry up" and "Let's go" are examples of commands commonly used by dog owners. Get in the habit of giving the puppy your chosen relief command before you take him out. That way, when he becomes an adult, you will be able to determine if he wants to go out when you ask him. A confirmation will be signs of interest like wagging his tail, watching you intently, going to the door, etc.

PUPPY'S NEEDS
The puppy needs to relieve himself after play periods, after each meal, after he has been

sleeping and at any time he indicates that he is looking for a place to urinate or defecate. The urinary and intestinal tract muscles of very young puppies are not fully developed. Therefore, like human babies, puppies need to relieve themselves frequently.

Take your puppy out often—every hour for an eight-week-old, for example—and always immediately after sleeping and eating. The older the puppy, the less often he will need to relieve himself. Finally, as a mature healthy adult, he will require only three to five relief trips per day.

HOUSING
Since the types of housing and control you provide for your puppy have a direct relationship on the success of house-training, we consider the various aspects of both before we begin training.

Taking a new puppy home and turning him loose in your house can be compared to turning a child loose in a sports arena and telling the child that the place is all his! The sheer enormity of the place would be too much for him to handle. Instead, offer the puppy clearly defined areas where he can play, sleep, eat and live. A room of the house where the family gathers is the most obvious choice. Puppies are social animals and need to feel a part of the pack right from the start. Hearing your

CANINE DEVELOPMENT SCHEDULE

It is important to understand how and at what age a puppy develops into adulthood.
If you are a puppy owner, consult the following Canine Development Schedule to
determine the stage of development your puppy is currently experiencing.
This knowledge will help you as you work with the puppy in the weeks and months ahead.

Period	Age	Characteristics
FIRST TO THIRD	BIRTH TO SEVEN WEEKS	Puppy needs food, sleep and warmth, and responds to simple and gentle touching. Needs mother for security and disciplining. Needs littermates for learning and interacting with other dogs. Pup learns to function within a pack and learns pack order of dominance. Begin socializing pup with adults and children for short periods. Pup begins to become aware of his environment.
FOURTH	EIGHT TO TWELVE WEEKS	Brain is fully developed. Needs socializing with outside world. Remove from mother and littermates. Needs to change from canine pack to human pack. Human dominance necessary. Fear period occurs between 8 and 12 weeks. Avoid fright and pain.
FIFTH	THIRTEEN TO SIXTEEN WEEKS	Training and formal obedience should begin. Less association with other dogs, more with people, places, situations. Period will pass easily if you remember this is pup's change-to-adolescence time. Be firm and fair. Flight instinct prominent. Permissiveness and over-disciplining can do permanent damage. Praise for good behavior.
JUVENILE	FOUR TO EIGHT MONTHS	Another fear period about 7 to 8 months of age. It passes quickly, but be cautious of fright and pain. Sexual maturity reached. Dominant traits established. Dog should understand sit, down, come and stay by now.

NOTE: THESE ARE APPROXIMATE TIME FRAMES. ALLOW FOR INDIVIDUAL DIFFERENCES IN PUPPIES.

voice, watching you while you are doing things and smelling you nearby are all positive reinforcers that he is now a member of your pack. Usually a family room, the kitchen or a nearby adjoining breakfast area is ideal for providing safety and security for both puppy and owner.

Within the designated room, there should be a smaller area that the puppy can call his own. An alcove or a partitioned (not boarded!) corner from which he can view the activities of his new family will be fine. The size of the area is the key factor here. The area must be large enough so that the puppy can lie down and stretch out, as well as stand up, without rubbing his head on the top. The pup should be taken out often to relieve himself so that he is not forced to soil his area when he can no longer "hold it." This is the basis of house-training. Dogs are, by nature, clean animals and will not remain close to their relief areas unless forced to do so. In those cases, they then become dirty dogs and usually remain that way for life.

The dog's designated area should contain clean bedding and a toy. Water must always be available, in a non-spill container, during house-training, although you'll want to be aware of when your pup is drinking water so you can predict when he will need to "go."

ATTENTION!
Your dog is actually training you at the same time you are training him. Dogs do things to get attention. They usually repeat whatever succeeds in getting your attention.

CONTROL

By control, we mean helping the puppy to create a lifestyle pattern that will be compatible to that of his human pack (*you*!). Just as we guide little children to learn our way of life, we must show the puppy when it is time to play, eat, sleep, exercise and even entertain himself.

Your puppy should always sleep in his designated area, whether this be a puppy pen or a room or area especially prepared for that purpose. He should also learn that, during times of household confusion and excessive human activity, such as at breakfast when family members are preparing for the day, he can play by himself in relative safety and comfort in his designated area. Each time you leave the puppy alone, he should understand exactly where he is to stay.

Puppies are chewers. They cannot tell the difference between lamp cords, television wires, shoes, table legs, etc. Chewing into a television wire, for example, can be fatal to the puppy, while a shorted wire can start a fire in the house. If the puppy chews on the arm of the chair when he is alone, you will probably discipline him angrily when you get home. Thus, he makes the association that your coming home means he is going to be punished. (He will not remember chewing the chair and is incapable of making the association of the discipline with his naughty deed.) Accustoming the pup to his designated area not only keeps him safe but also avoids his engaging in destructive behaviors when you are not around.

Times of excitement, such as special occasions, family parties, etc., can be fun for the puppy, providing that he can view the activities from the security of his designated area. He is not underfoot and he is not being fed all sorts of tidbits that will probably cause him stomach distress, yet he still feels a part of the fun.

ESTABLISHING A SCHEDULE

A puppy should be taken to his relief area each time he is released from his designated area, after meals, after play sessions and when he first awakens in the morning (at age eight weeks, this can mean 5 a.m.!). The puppy will indicate that he's ready "to go" by circling or sniffing busily—do not misinterpret these signs. For a puppy less than ten weeks of age, a routine of taking him out every

hour is necessary. As the puppy grows, he will be able to wait for longer periods of time.

Keep trips to his relief area short. Stay no more than five or six minutes and then return to the house. If he goes during that time, praise him lavishly and take him

HOW MANY TIMES A DAY?

AGE	RELIEF TRIPS
To 14 weeks	10
14–22 weeks	8
22–32 weeks	6
Adulthood	4
(dog stops growing)	

These are estimates, of course, but they are a guide to the *minimum* number of opportunities a dog should have each day to relieve himself.

indoors immediately. If he does not, but he has an accident when you go back indoors, say "No! No!" and return to his relief area. Wait a few minutes, then return to the house again. Never hit a puppy or put his face in urine or excrement when he has had an accident!

Once indoors, put the puppy in his special area until you have had time to clean up his accident. Then, release him to the family area and watch him more closely than before. Chances are, his accident was a result of your not picking up his signal or waiting too long before offering him the opportunity to relieve himself. Never hold a grudge against the puppy for accidents.

Let the puppy learn that going outdoors means it is time to relieve himself, not to play. Once trained, he will be able to play indoors and out and still differentiate between the times for play versus the times for relief.

Help him develop regular hours for naps, being alone, playing by himself and just resting, all in his own area. Encourage him to entertain himself while you are busy with your activities. Let him learn that having you near is comforting, but it is not your main purpose in life to provide him with undivided attention.

Each time you put your puppy in his own area, use the same command, whatever suits best.

Soon he will run to his special area when he hears you say those words.

In conclusion, a few key elements are really all you need for a successful house-training method—consistency, frequency, praise, control and supervision. By following these procedures with a normal, healthy puppy, you and the puppy will soon be past the stage of accidents and ready to move on to a clean and rewarding life together.

ROLES OF DISCIPLINE, REWARD AND PUNISHMENT

Discipline, training one to act in accordance with rules, brings order to life. It is as simple as that. Without discipline, particularly in a group society, chaos will reign supreme and the group will eventually perish. Humans and canines are social animals and need some form of discipline in order to function effectively. They must procure food, reproduce to keep their species going and protect their home base and their young. If there were no discipline in the lives of social animals, they would eventually die from starvation and/or predation by other stronger animals. In the case of domestic canines, discipline in their lives is needed in order for them to understand how their pack (you and other family members) functions and how they must act in order to survive.

A large humane society in an highly populated area recently surveyed dog owners regarding their satisfaction with their relationships with their dogs. People who had trained their dogs were 75% more satisfied with their pets than those who had never trained their dogs.

Dr. Edward Thorndike, a noted psychologist, established *Thorndike's Theory of Learning*, which states that a behavior that results in a pleasant event tends to be repeated. Likewise, a behavior that results in an unpleasant event tends not to be repeated. It is this theory upon which training methods are based today. For example, if you manipulate a dog to perform a specific behavior and reward him for doing it, he is likely to do it again because he enjoyed the end result.

Occasionally, punishment, a penalty inflicted for an offense, is necessary. The best type of punishment often comes from an outside source. For example, a child is told not to touch the stove because he may get burned. He disobeys and touches the stove. In doing so, he receives a burn. From that time on, he respects the heat of the stove and avoids contact with it. Therefore, a behavior that results in an unpleasant event tends not to be repeated.

A good example of a dog learning the hard way is the dog who chases the house cat. He is told many times to leave the cat alone, yet he persists in teasing

FEAR AGGRESSION

Pups who are subjected to physical abuse during training commonly end up with behavioral problems as adults. One common result of abuse is fear aggression, in which a dog will lash out, bare his teeth, snarl and finally bite someone by whom he feels threatened. For example, your daughter may be playing with the dog one afternoon. As they play hide-and-seek, she backs the dog into a corner and, as she attempts to tease him playfully, he bites her hand. Examine the cause of this behavior. Did your daughter ever hit the dog? Did someone who resembles your daughter hit or scream at the dog?

Fortunately, fear aggression is relatively easy to correct. Have your daughter engage in only positive activities with the dog, such as feeding, petting and walking. She should not give any corrections or negative feedback. If the dog still growls or cowers away from her, allow someone else to accompany them. After approximately one week, the dog should feel that he can rely on her for many positive things, and he will also be prevented from reacting fearfully towards anyone who might resemble her.

the cat. Then, one day, the dog begins chasing the cat but the cat turns and swipes a claw across the dog's face, leaving the dog with a painful gash on his nose. The final result is that the dog stops chasing the cat.

TRAINING EQUIPMENT

COLLAR AND LEAD
For a Mastiff, the collar and lead that you use for training must be one with which you are easily able to work and perfectly safe.

TREATS
Have a bag of treats on hand; something nutritious and easy to swallow works best. Use a soft treat, a chunk of cheese or a piece of cooked chicken rather than a dry biscuit. Using food rewards will not teach a dog to beg at the table—the only way to teach a dog to beg at the table is to give him food from the table. In training, rewarding the dog with a food treat will help him associate praise and the treats with learning new behaviors that obviously please his owner.

TRAINING BEGINS: ASK THE DOG A QUESTION
In order to teach your dog anything, you must first get his attention. After all, he cannot learn anything if he is looking away from you with his mind on something else.

To get your dog's attention, ask him "School?" and immediately walk over to him and give him a treat as you tell him "Good dog." Wait a minute or two and repeat the routine, this time with a treat in your hand as you approach within a foot of the dog. Do not go directly to him, but stop about a foot short of him and hold

CALM DOWN
Dogs will do anything for your attention. If you reward the dog when he is calm and attentive, you will develop a well-mannered dog. If, on the other hand, you greet your dog excitedly and encourage him to wrestle with you, the dog will greet you the same way and you will have a hyperactive dog on your hands.

out the treat as you ask "School?" He will see you approaching with a treat in your hand and most likely begin walking toward you. As you meet, give him the treat and praise again.

The third time, ask the question, have a treat in your hand and walk only a short distance toward the dog so that he must walk almost all the way to you. As he reaches you, give him the treat and praise again.

By this time, the dog will probably be getting the idea that if he pays attention to you, especially when you ask that question, it will pay off in treats and enjoyable activities for him. In other words, he learns that "school" means doing great things with you that are fun and that result in positive attention for him.

Remember that the dog does not understand your verbal language; he only recognizes sounds. Your question translates to a series of sounds for him, and those sounds become the signal to go to you and pay attention. The dog learns that if he does this, he will get to interact with you plus receive treats and praise.

THE BASIC COMMANDS

TEACHING SIT

Now that you have the dog's attention, attach his lead and hold it in your left hand, and hold a food treat in your right hand.

SAFETY FIRST
While it may seem that the most important things to your dog are eating, sleeping and chewing the upholstery on your furniture, his first concern is actually safety. The domesticated dogs we keep as companions have the same pack instinct as their ancestors who ran free thousands of years ago. Because of this pack instinct, your dog wants to know that he and his pack are not in danger of being harmed, and that his pack has a strong, capable leader. You must establish yourself as the leader early on in your relationship. That way your dog will trust that you will take care of him and the pack, and he will accept your commands without question.

Place your food hand at the dog's nose and let him lick the treat but not take it from you. Say "Sit" and slowly raise your food hand from in front of the dog's nose up over his head so that he is looking at the ceiling. As he bends his head upward, he will have to bend his knees to maintain his balance. As he bends his knees, he will assume a sit position. At that point, release the food treat and praise lavishly with comments such as "Good dog! Good sit!," etc. Remember to always praise enthusiastically,

Once your Mastiffs are trained, you can practice commands in a variety of locations. Until then, train your Mastiff one-on-one in a secure location that is devoid of distractions.

because dogs relish verbal praise from their owners and feel so proud of themselves whenever they accomplish a behavior.

Incidentally, you will not use food forever in getting the dog to obey your commands. Food is only used to teach new behaviors and, once the dog knows what you want when you give a specific command, you will wean him off the food treats but still maintain the verbal praise. After all, you will always have your voice with you, and there will be many times when you have no food rewards but expect the dog to obey.

TEACHING DOWN

Teaching the down exercise is easy when you understand how the dog perceives the down position, and it is very difficult when you do not. Dogs perceive the down position as a submissive one; therefore, teaching the down exercise by using a forceful method can sometimes make the dog develop such a fear of the down that he either runs away when you say "Down" or he attempts to snap at the person who tries to force him down.

Have the dog sit close alongside your left leg, facing in the same direction as you are. Hold the lead in your left hand and a food treat in your right. Now place your left hand lightly on the top of the dog's shoulders where they meet above the spinal cord. Do not push down on the dog's shoulders; simply rest your left hand there so you can guide the dog to lie down close to your left leg rather than to swing away from your side when he drops.

Now place the food hand at the dog's nose, say "Down" very softly (almost a whisper) and slowly lower the food hand to the dog's front feet. When the food hand reaches the floor, begin moving it forward along the floor in front of the dog. Keep talking softly to the dog, saying things like, "Do you want this treat? You can do this, good dog." Your reassuring tone of voice will help calm the dog as he tries to follow the food hand in order to get the treat.

When the dog's elbows touch the floor, release the food and praise softly. Try to get the dog to maintain that down position for several seconds before you let him sit up again. The goal here is to get the dog to settle down and not feel threatened in the down position.

TEACHING STAY

It is easy to teach the dog to stay in either a sit or a down position. Again, we use food and praise during the teaching process as we help the dog to understand exactly what it is that we are expecting him to do.

To teach the sit/stay, start with the dog sitting on your left side as before and hold the lead in your left hand. Have a food treat in your right hand and place your food hand at the dog's nose. Say "Stay" and step out on your right foot to stand directly in front of the dog, toe to toe, as he licks and nibbles the treat. Be sure to keep his head facing upward to maintain the sit position. Count to five and then swing around to stand next to the dog again with him on your left. As soon as you get back to the original position, release the food and praise lavishly.

To teach the down/stay, do the down as previously described.

DOUBLE JEOPARDY

A dog in jeopardy never lies down. He stays alert on his feet because instinct tells him that he may have to run away or fight for his survival. Therefore, if a dog feels threatened or anxious, he will not lie down. Consequently, it is important to keep the dog calm and relaxed as he learns the down exercise.

As soon as the dog lies down, say "Stay" and step out on your right foot just as you did in the sit/stay. Count to five and then return to stand beside the dog with him on your left side. Release the treat and praise as always.

Within a week or ten days, you can begin to add a bit of distance between you and your dog when you leave him. When you do, use your left hand open with the palm facing the dog as a stay signal, much the same as the hand signal a police officer uses to stop traffic at an intersection. Hold the food treat in your right hand as before, but this time the

CONSISTENCY PAYS OFF

Dogs need consistency in their feeding schedule, exercise and relief visits, and in the verbal commands you use. If you use "Stay" on Monday and "Stay here, please" on Tuesday, you will confuse your dog. Don't demand perfect behavior during training sessions and then let him have the run of the house the rest of the day. Above all, lavish praise on your pet consistently every time he does something right. The more he feels he is pleasing you, the more willing he will be to learn.

food will not be touching the dog's nose. He will watch the food hand and quickly learn that he is going to get that treat as soon as you return to his side.

When you can stand 3 feet away from your dog for 30 seconds, you can then begin building time and distance in both stays. Eventually, the dog can be expected to remain in the stay position for prolonged periods of time until you return to him or call him to you. Always praise lavishly when he stays.

TEACHING COME

If you make teaching "come" an exciting experience, you should never have a student that does not love the game or that fails to come when called. The secret, it seems, is never to teach the word "come."

At times when an owner most wants his dog to come when called, the owner is likely to be upset or anxious and he allows these feelings to come through in the tone of his voice when he calls his dog. Hearing that desperation in his owner's voice, the dog fears the results of going to him and therefore either disobeys outright or runs in the opposite direction. The secret, therefore, is to teach the dog a game and, when you want him to come to you, simply play the game. It is practically a no-fail solution!

To begin, have several members of your family take a few food treats and each go into a different room in the house. Everyone takes turns calling the dog, and each person should celebrate the dog's finding him with a treat and lots of happy praise. When a person calls the dog, he is actually inviting the dog to find him and to get a treat as a reward for "winning."

A few turns of the "Where are you?" game and the dog will understand that everyone is playing the game and that each person has a big celebration awaiting the dog's success at locating him or her. Once the dog learns to love the game, simply calling out "Where are you?" will bring him running from wherever he is when he hears that all-important question. Do not overdo this exercise or you may exhaust your Mastiff puppy. Practice it only two or three times each day.

The come command is recognized as one of the most important things to teach a dog, but there are trainers who work with thousands of dogs and never teach the actual word "come." Yet these dogs will respond to a person who uses the dog's name followed by "Where are you?" For example, a woman has a 10-year-old companion dog who went blind, but who never fails to locate her owner when asked, "Where are you?"

"COME" . . . BACK

Never call your dog to come to you for a correction or scold him when he reaches you. That is the quickest way to turn a come command into "Go away fast!" Dogs think only in the present tense, and your dog will connect the scolding with coming to you, not with the misbehavior of a few moments earlier.

to heel when you can't stop him in his tracks.

Begin by holding the lead in your left hand as the dog sits beside your left leg. Move the loop end of the lead to your right hand, but keep your left hand short on the lead so that it keeps the dog in close next to you.

Say "Heel" and step forward on your left foot. Keep the dog close to you and take three steps. Stop and have the dog sit next to you in what we now call the heel position. Praise verbally, but do not touch the dog. Hesitate a moment and begin again with "Heel," taking three steps and stopping, at which point the dog is told to sit again.

Your goal here is to have the dog walk those three steps without pulling on the lead. Once he will walk calmly beside you for three steps without pulling, increase the number of steps you take to five. When he will walk politely beside you while you take five steps, you can increase the length of your walk to ten steps. Keep increasing the length of your

TEACHING HEEL

Heeling means that the dog walks beside the owner without pulling. It takes time and patience on the owner's part to succeed at teaching the dog that he (the owner) will not proceed unless the dog is walking calmly beside him. Neither pulling out ahead on the lead nor lagging behind is acceptable. Since Mastiff owners do not have the need to walk their dogs too frequently during the first year of life, this command may not seem imperative to teach right away. True, and not true. Although you will not be walking the dog great distances, you do not want to be pulled around on a short walk either. Once the dog is six months old (and weighs as much as you do!), it will be more difficult to convince your Mastiff

EASY DOES IT

Gently laying your hand over the top of the dog's neck right behind the ears acts as a dominant signal. Adding a soothing, soft voice with the word "easy" can calm an overly excited dog and help him resume a normal attitude.

stroll until the dog will walk quietly beside you without pulling as long as you want him to heel. When you stop heeling, indicate to the dog that the exercise is over by verbally praising as you pet him and say "OK, good dog." The "OK" is used as a release word, meaning that the exercise is finished and the dog is free to relax.

If you are dealing with a pup who insists on pulling you around, simply "put on your brakes" and stand your ground until the dog realizes that the two of you are not going anywhere until he is beside you and moving at your pace, not his. It may take some time just standing there to convince the dog that you are the leader and that you will be the one to decide on the direction and speed of your travel.

Each time the dog looks up at you or slows down to give a

When training a dog as giant as the Mastiff, heeling is an absolute necessity. Your Mastiff must heed your command at all times, or else *you* will be taken for quite a walk!

slack lead between the two of you, quietly praise him and say, "Good heel. Good dog." Eventually, the dog will begin to respond and within a few days he will be walking politely beside you without pulling on the lead. At first, the training sessions should be kept short and very positive; soon the dog will be able to walk nicely with you for increasingly longer distances. Remember also to give the dog free time and the opportunity to play when you have finished heel practice.

WEANING OFF FOOD IN TRAINING

Food is used in training new behaviors. Once the dog understands what behavior goes with a specific command, it is time to start weaning him off the food treats. At first, give a treat after each exercise. Then, start to give a treat only after every other exercise. Mix up the times when you offer a food reward and the times when you only offer praise so that the dog will never know when he is going to receive both food and praise and when he is going to receive only praise. This is called a variable-ratio reward system. It proves successful because there is always the chance that the owner will produce a treat, so the dog never stops trying for that reward. No matter what, *always* give verbal praise.

HELPING PAWS
Your dog may not be the next Lassie, but every pet has the potential to do some tricks well. Identify his natural talents and hone them. Is your dog always happy and upbeat? Teach him to wag his tail or give you his paw on command. Real homebodies can be trained to do household chores, such as carrying dirty laundry or retrieving the morning paper.

OBEDIENCE CLASSES

I've already mentioned that it is a good idea to enroll in an obedience class if one is available in your area. If yours is a show dog, classes to prepare for the show ring would be more appropriate. Many areas have dog clubs that offer basic obedience training as well as preparatory classes for obedience competition. There are also local dog trainers who offer similar classes.

At obedience trials, dogs can earn titles at various levels of competition. The beginning levels of obedience competition include basic behaviors such as sit, down, heel, etc. The more advanced levels of competition include jumping, retrieving, scent discrimination and signal work. The advanced levels require a dog and owner to put a lot of time and effort into their training. The titles that can be earned at these levels of competition are very prestigious.

Dogs suffer from many of the same physical illnesses as people and might even share many of the same psychological problems. Since people usually know more about human diseases than canine maladies, many of the terms used in this chapter will be familiar but not necessarily those used by veterinarians. For example, we will use the familiar term *x-ray* instead of *radiograph*. We will also use the familiar term *symptoms*, even though dogs don't have symptoms, which are verbal descriptions of something the patient feels or observes himself that he regards as abnormal. Dogs have *clinical signs* since they cannot speak, so we have to look for these clinical signs...but we still use the term *symptoms* in the book.

Medicine is a constantly changing art, with of course scientific input as well. Things alter as we learn more and more about basic sciences such as genetics and biochemistry, and have use of more sophisticated imaging techniques like Computer Aided Tomography (CAT scans) or Magnetic Resonance Imaging (MRI scans). There is academic dispute about many canine maladies, so different vets treat them in different ways. For example, some vets place a greater emphasis on surgical treatment than others.

SELECTING A VETERINARIAN
Your selection of a veterinarian should be based on personal recommendation for his skills with large-breed dogs, and, if possible, the Mastiff. If the vet is based nearby, it will be helpful because you might have an emergency or need to make multiple visits for treatments.

All veterinarians are licensed and should be capable of dealing with routine medical issues such as infections, injuries, routine surgeries (like neutering and stitching up wounds) and the promotion of health (for example, by vaccination). If the problem affecting your dog is more complex, your vet will refer your pet to someone with a more detailed knowledge of what is wrong. This will usually be a specialist who concentrates in a specific field of veterinary medicine.

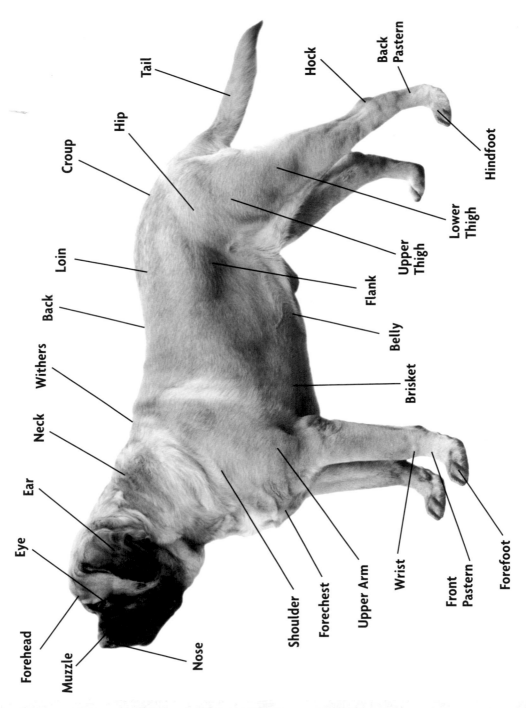

PHYSICAL STRUCTURE OF THE MASTIFF

Tail

Hock

Back
Pastern

Hip

Croup

Hindfoot

Loin

Lower
Thigh

Upper
Thigh

Back

Flank

Withers

Belly

Neck

Brisket

Ear

Eye

Forehead

Muzzle

Nose

Shoulder

Forechest

Upper Arm

Wrist

Front
Pastern

Forefoot

Veterinary procedures are very costly and, as the treatments available improve, they are going to become more expensive. It is quite acceptable to discuss matters of cost with your vet; if there is more than one treatment option, cost may be a factor in deciding which route to take. It is also acceptable to get a second opinion, although it is courteous to advise the vets concerned that you are doing so.

Insurance against veterinary cost is also becoming very popular. The extent of coverage can range from that for emergencies only to policies that also cover aspects of your dog's routine health care. Discuss this with your vet.

PREVENTATIVE MEDICINE
It is much easier, less costly and more effective to practice preventative medicine than to fight bouts of illness and disease. Properly bred puppies of all breeds come from parents that were selected based upon their genetic-disease profiles. The puppies' mother should have been vaccinated, free of all internal and external parasites and properly nourished. For these reasons, a visit to the veterinarian who cared for the dam is recommended if at all possible. The dam passes disease resistance to her puppies, which should last from eight to ten weeks. Unfortunately, she can also pass

on parasites and infection. This is why knowledge about her health is useful in learning more about the health of the puppies.

WEANING TO BRINGING PUP HOME
Puppies should be weaned by the time they are two months old. A puppy that remains for at least eight weeks with his mother and littermates usually adapts better to other dogs and people later in life.

Some new owners have their puppy examined by a veterinarian immediately, which is a good idea unless the puppy is overtired by a long journey. In that case, an appointment should be arranged for the next day.

Your Mastiff's vet will have a lot of dog to deal with! A vet who specializes in large breeds will be better equipped to deal with your dog's special needs.

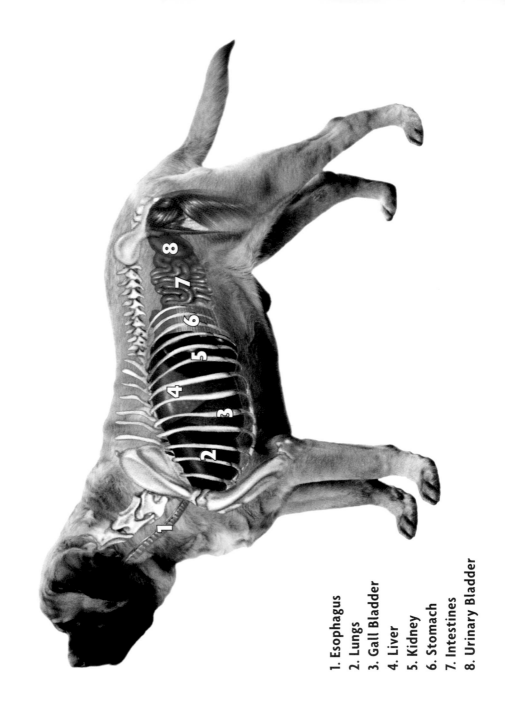

1. Esophagus
2. Lungs
3. Gall Bladder
4. Liver
5. Kidney
6. Stomach
7. Intestines
8. Urinary Bladder

INTERNAL ORGANS OF THE MASTIFF

The puppy will have his teeth examined and have his skeletal conformation and general health checked prior to certification by the veterinarian. Puppies in certain breeds have problems with their kneecaps, cataracts and other eye problems, heart murmurs and undescended testicles. Your veterinarian might have training in temperament testing and evaluation. At the first visit, the vet will set up a schedule for your pup's vaccinations.

VACCINATION PROGRAMS

Most vaccinations are given by injection and should only be given by a veterinarian. Both he and you should keep a record of the date of the injection, the identification of the vaccine and the amount given. Some vets give a first vaccination at six weeks, but most dog breeders prefer the course not to commence until about eight weeks because of the risk of interaction with the antibodies produced by the mother. The vaccination schedule is usually based on a two- to four-week cycle. You must take your vet's advice as to when to vaccinate, as this may differ according to the vaccine used.

The usual vaccines contain immunizing doses of several different viruses such as distemper, parvovirus, parainfluenza and

HEALTH AND VACCINATION SCHEDULE

AGE IN WEEKS:	6TH	8TH	10TH	12TH	14TH	16TH	20-24TH	52ND
Worm Control	✔	✔	✔	✔	✔	✔	✔	
Neutering							✔	
Heartworm		✔		✔		✔	✔	
Parvovirus			✔		✔		✔	✔
Distemper		✔		✔		✔		✔
Hepatitis		✔		✔		✔		✔
Leptospirosis								✔
Parainfluenza			✔		✔			✔
Dental Examination		✔					✔	✔
Complete Physical		✔					✔	✔
Coronavirus				✔			✔	✔
Canine Cough								
Hip Dysplasia							✔	
Rabies							✔	

Vaccinations are not instantly effective. It takes about two weeks for the dog's immune system to develop antibodies. Most vaccinations require annual booster shots. Your veterinarian should guide you in this regard.

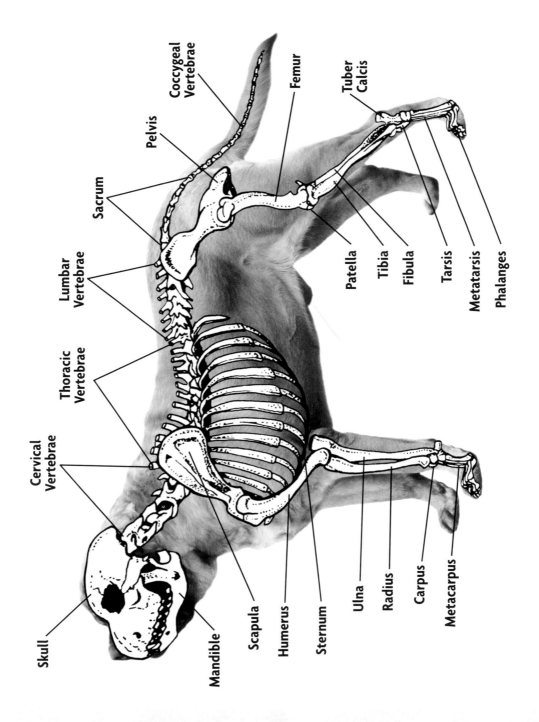

Coccygeal Vertebrae

Femur

Tuber Calcis

Pelvis

Sacrum

Lumbar Vertebrae

Thoracic Vertebrae

Cervical Vertebrae

Patella

Tibia

Fibula

Tarsis

Metatarsis

Phalanges

Skull

Mandible

Scapula

Humerus

Sternum

Ulna

Radius

Carpus

Metacarpus

SKELETAL STRUCTURE OF THE MASTIFF

DISEASE REFERENCE CHART

	What is it?	What causes it?	Symptoms
Leptospirosis	Severe disease that affects the internal organs; can be spread to people.	A bacterium, which is often carried by rodents, that enters through mucous membranes and spreads quickly throughout the body.	Range from fever, vomiting and loss of appetite in less severe cases to shock, irreversible kidney damage and possibly death in most severe cases.
Rabies	Potentially deadly virus that infects warm-blooded mammals.	Bite from a carrier of the virus, mainly wild animals.	1st stage: dog exhibits change in behavior, fear. 2nd stage: dog's behavior becomes more aggressive. 3rd stage: loss of coordination, trouble with bodily functions.
Parvovirus	Highly contagious virus, potentially deadly.	Ingestion of the virus, which is usually spread through the feces of infected dogs.	Most common: severe diarrhea. Also vomiting, fatigue, lack of appetite.
Canine cough	Contagious respiratory infection.	Combination of types of bacteria and virus. Most common: *Bordetella bronchiseptica* bacteria and parainfluenza virus.	Chronic cough.
Distemper	Disease primarily affecting respiratory and nervous system.	Virus that is related to the human measles virus.	Mild symptoms such as fever, lack of appetite and mucus secretion progress to evidence of brain damage, "hard pad."
Hepatitis	Virus primarily affecting the liver.	Canine adenovirus type I (CAV-1). Enters system when dog breathes in particles.	Lesser symptoms include listlessness, diarrhea, vomiting. More severe symptoms include "blue-eye" (clumps of virus in eye).
Coronavirus	Virus resulting in digestive problems.	Virus is spread through infected dog's feces.	Stomach upset evidenced by lack of appetite, vomiting, diarrhea.

hepatitis. There are other vaccines available when the puppy is at risk. You should rely upon professional advice. This is especially true for the booster immunizations. Most vaccination programs require a booster when the puppy is a year old and once a year thereafter. In some cases, circumstances may require more or less frequent immunizations.

Canine cough, more formally known as tracheobronchitis, is immunized against with a vaccine that is sprayed into the dog's nostrils. Canine cough is usually included in routine vaccination, but it is often not as effective as the vaccines for other diseases.

FIVE MONTHS TO ONE YEAR OF AGE
Unless you intend to breed or show your dog, neutering the puppy around six months of age is recommended. Discuss this with your veterinarian. Neutering/spaying has proven to be extremely beneficial to male and female dogs, respectively. Besides eliminating the possibility of pregnancy and pyometra in bitches and testicular cancer in males, it greatly reduces the risk of breast cancer in bitches and prostate cancer in males.

Your veterinarian should provide your puppy with a thorough dental evaluation at six months of age, ascertaining

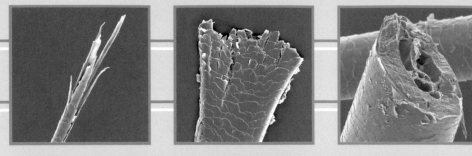

Normal hairs of a dog, enlarged 200 times original size. The cuticle (outer covering) is clean and healthy. Unlike human hair that grows from the base, a dog's hair also grows from the end. Damaged hairs and split ends, illustrated above.

whether all of the permanent teeth have erupted properly. A home dental-care regimen should be initiated at six months, including brushing weekly and providing good dental devices (such as nylon bones). Regular dental care promotes healthy teeth, fresh breath and a longer life. Don't forget to give your Mastiff an apple a day to keep the veterinary dentist away!

DOGS OLDER THAN ONE YEAR
Continue to visit the veterinarian at least once a year for complete check-ups. There is no such disease as "old age," but bodily functions do change with age. The eyes and ears are no longer as efficient. Liver, kidney and intestinal functions often decline. Proper dietary changes, recommended by your veterinarian, can make life more pleasant for your aging Mastiff and you.

SKIN PROBLEMS
Veterinarians are consulted by dog owners for skin problems more than for any other group of diseases or maladies. A dog's skin is as sensitive, if not more so, than human skin, and both can suffer from almost the same ailments (including every teenager's most hated problem: acne!). For this reason, veterinary dermatology has developed into a specialty practiced by many vets.

Since many skin problems have visual symptoms that are almost identical, it requires the skill of an experienced veterinary dermatologist to identify and cure many of the more severe skin disorders. Pet shops sell many treatments for skin problems, but most of the treatments are directed at symptoms and not at the underlying problem(s). If your dog is suffering from a skin disorder, you should seek professional assistance as quickly as possible. As with all diseases, the earlier a problem is identified and treated, the more likely it is that the cure will be successful.

ACNE
Although acne is rare in most dogs, the Mastiff has bouts of acne just like teenage humans. Acne is very usual in young Mastiffs, between the ages of 4 and 18 months. It appears in both dogs and bitches and, like human acne, is directly related to hormonal activity. These unattractive pimples usually appear during the rapid-growth stages, the pup's transition from puppyhood to puberty. In the case of bitches, pimples usually appear immediately before a heat period, or during pregnancy, whelping and lactation. Acne breaks out in the area surrounding the chin or the lips and in the lateral sides of the flews.

Although some people recommend the use of anti-inflammatory products with cortisone, I personally do not feel that such treatment is necessary. Acne is a natural process that only occurs under specific conditions and is a fairly controlled problem. Fortunately, owners don't have to deal with the embarrassment that usually accompanies these unsightly pimples. No one is going to tease your Mastiff pup at obedience school!

It is recommended that the owner clean the affected area twice or three times a day with hydrogen peroxide on a piece of gauze. Never use cotton balls or pads, as the fibers tend to adhere to the blemishes. If the pimples erupt and begin to look infected, a few drops of Betadine should be immediately applied. In a few days, the acne will have disappeared without leaving any further trace.

ACRAL LICK GRANULOMA

Many large dogs have a very poorly understood syndrome called acral lick granuloma. The manifestation of the problem is the dog's tireless attack at a specific area of the body, almost always the leg or paw. The dog licks so intensively that he removes the hair and skin, leaving an ugly, large wound. Tiny protuberances, which are outgrowths of new capillaries, bead on the surface of the wound. Owners who notice their dogs' biting and chewing at their extremities should have the vet determine the cause. If lick granuloma is identified, although there is no absolute cure, corticosteroids are one common treatment.

AUTO-IMMUNE ILLNESSES

An auto-immune illness is one in which the immune system overacts and does not recognize parts of the affected person; rather, the immune system starts to react as if these parts were foreign and need to be destroyed. An example is rheumatoid arthritis, which occurs when the body does not recognize the joints, thus leading to a very painful and damaging reaction in the joints. This has nothing to do with age, so can occur in children and young dogs. The wear-and-tear arthritis seen in the older person or dog is known as osteoarthritis.

Lupus is an auto-immune disease that affects dogs as well as people. It can take variable forms, affecting the kidneys, bones and the skin. It can be fatal, so is treated with steroids, which can themselves have very significant side effects. The steroids calm down the allergic reaction to the body's tissues, which helps the lupus, but they also decrease the body's reaction to real foreign substances such as bacteria, and also thin the skin and bone.

Number-One Killer Disease in Dogs: CANCER

In every age, there is a word associated with a disease or plague that causes humans to shudder. In the 21st century, that word is "cancer." Just as cancer is the leading cause of death in humans, it claims nearly half the lives of dogs that die from a natural disease as well as half the dogs that die over the age of ten years.

Described as a genetic disease, cancer becomes a greater risk as the dog ages. Vets and dog owners have become increasingly aware of the threat of cancer to dogs. Statistics reveal that one dog in every five will develop cancer, the most common of which is skin cancer. Many cancers, including prostate, ovarian and breast cancer, can be avoided by spaying and neutering our dogs by the age of six months.

Early detection of cancer can save or extend a dog's life, so it is absolutely vital for owners to have their dogs examined by a qualified vet or oncologist immediately upon detection of any abnormality. Certain dietary guidelines have also proven to reduce the onset and spread of cancer. Foods based on fish rather than beef, due to the presence of Omega-3 fatty acids, are recommended. Other amino acids such as glutamine have significant benefits for canines, particularly those breeds that show a greater susceptibility to cancer.

Cancer management and treatments promise hope for future generations of canines. Since the disease is genetic, breeders should never breed a dog whose parents, grandparents and any related siblings have developed cancer. It is difficult to know whether to exclude an otherwise healthy dog from a breeding program, as the disease does not manifest itself until the dog's senior years.

RECOGNIZE CANCER WARNING SIGNS

Since early detection can possibly rescue your dog from becoming a cancer statistic, it is essential for owners to recognize the possible signs and seek the assistance of a qualified professional.

- Abnormal bumps or lumps that continue to grow
- Bleeding or discharge from any body cavity
- Persistent stiffness or lameness
- Recurrent sores or sores that do not heal
- Inappetence
- Breathing difficulties
- Weight loss
- Bad breath or odors
- General malaise and fatigue
- Eating and swallowing problems
- Difficulty urinating and defecating

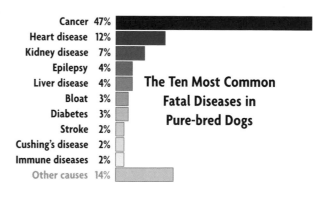

Cancer	47%
Heart disease	12%
Kidney disease	7%
Epilepsy	4%
Liver disease	4%
Bloat	3%
Diabetes	3%
Stroke	2%
Cushing's disease	2%
Immune diseases	2%
Other causes	14%

The Ten Most Common Fatal Diseases in Pure-bred Dogs

A male dog flea, *Ctenocephalides canis.*

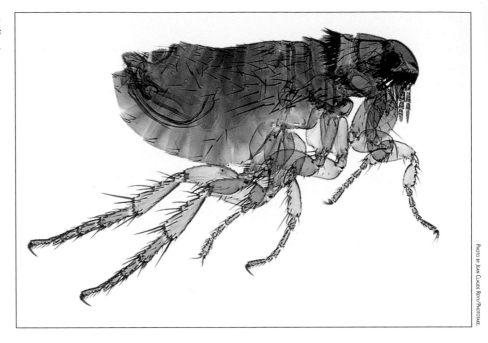

PHOTO BY JEAN CLAUDE REVY/PHOTOTAKE

EXTERNAL PARASITES

FLEAS

Of all the problems to which dogs are prone, none is more well known and frustrating than fleas. Flea infestation is relatively simple to cure but difficult to prevent. Parasites that are harbored inside the body are a bit more difficult to eradicate but they are easier to control.

To control flea infestation, you have to understand the flea's life cycle. Fleas are often thought of as a summertime problem, but centrally heated homes have changed the patterns and fleas can be found at any time of the year. The most effective method of flea control is a two-stage approach: one stage to kill the adult fleas, and the other to control the development of pre-adult fleas. Unfortunately, no single active ingredient is effective against all stages of the life cycle.

FLEA KILLER CAUTION— "POISON"

Flea-killers are poisonous. You should not spray these toxic chemicals on areas of a dog's body that he licks, including his genitals and his face. Flea killers taken internally are a better answer, but check with your vet in case internal therapy is not advised for your dog.

LIFE CYCLE STAGES

During its life, a flea will pass through four life stages: egg, larva, pupa or nymph and adult. The adult stage is the most visible and irritating stage of the flea life cycle, and this is why the majority of flea-control products concentrate on this stage. The fact is that adult fleas account for only 1% of the total flea population, and the other 99% exist in pre-adult stages, i.e. eggs, larvae and nymphs. The pre-adult stages are barely visible to the naked eye.

THE LIFE CYCLE OF THE FLEA

Eggs are laid on the dog, usually in quantities of about 20 or 30, several times a day. The adult female flea must have a blood meal before each egg-laying session. When first laid, the eggs will cling to the dog's hair, as the eggs are still moist. However, they will quickly dry out and fall from the dog, especially if the dog moves around or scratches. Many eggs will fall off in the dog's favorite area or an area in which he spends a lot of time, such as his bed.

Once the eggs fall from the dog onto the carpet or furniture, they will hatch into larvae. This takes from one to ten days. Larvae are not particularly mobile and will usually travel only a few inches from where they hatch. However, they do have a tendency to move away from bright light and heavy

EN GARDE:
CATCHING FLEAS OFF GUARD!
Consider the following ways to arm yourself against fleas:
• Add a small amount of pennyroyal or eucalyptus oil to your dog's bath. These natural remedies repel fleas.
• Supplement your dog's food with fresh garlic (minced or grated) and a hearty amount of brewer's yeast, both of which ward off fleas.
• Use a flea comb on your dog daily. Submerge fleas in a cup of bleach to kill them quickly.
• Confine the dog to only a few rooms to limit the spread of fleas in the home.
• Vacuum daily...and get all of the crevices! Dispose of the bag every few days until the problem is under control.
• Wash your dog's bedding daily. Cover cushions where your dog sleeps with towels, and wash the towels often.

traffic—under furniture and behind doors are common places to find high quantities of flea larvae.

The flea larvae feed on dead organic matter, including adult flea feces, until they are ready to change into adult fleas. Fleas will usually remain as larvae for around seven days. After this period, the larvae will pupate into protective pupae. While inside the pupae, the larvae will undergo

Fleas have been measured as being able to jump 300,000 times and can jump over 150 times their length in any direction, including straight up.

metamorphosis and change into adult fleas. This can take as little time as a few days, but the adult fleas can remain inside the pupae waiting to hatch for up to two years. The pupae are signaled to hatch by certain stimuli, such as physical pressure—the pupae's being stepped on, heat from an animal's lying on the pupae or increased carbon-dioxide levels and vibrations—indicating that a suitable host is available.

Once hatched, the adult flea must feed within a few days. Once the adult flea finds a host, it will not leave voluntarily. It only becomes dislodged by grooming or the host animal's scratching.

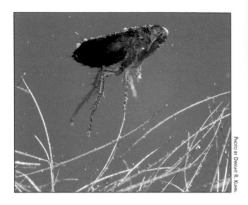

PHOTO BY DR DWIGHT R. KUHN

The adult flea will remain on the host for the duration of its life unless forcibly removed.

TREATING THE ENVIRONMENT AND THE DOG

Treating fleas should be a two-pronged attack. First, the environment needs to be treated; this includes carpets and furniture, especially the dog's bedding and areas underneath furniture. The environment should be treated with a household spray containing an Insect Growth Regulator (IGR) and an insecticide to kill the adult fleas. Most IGRs are effective against eggs and larvae; they actually mimic the fleas' own hormones and stop the eggs and larvae from developing into adult fleas. There are currently no treatments available to attack the pupa stage of the life cycle, so the adult insecticide is used to kill the newly hatched adult fleas before they find a host. Most IGRs are active for many months, while

A scanning electron micrograph of a dog or cat flea, *Ctenocephalides*, magnified more than 100x. This image has been colorized for effect.

S. E. M. BY DR DENNIS KUNKEL, UNIVERSITY OF HAWAII.

THE LIFE CYCLE OF THE FLEA

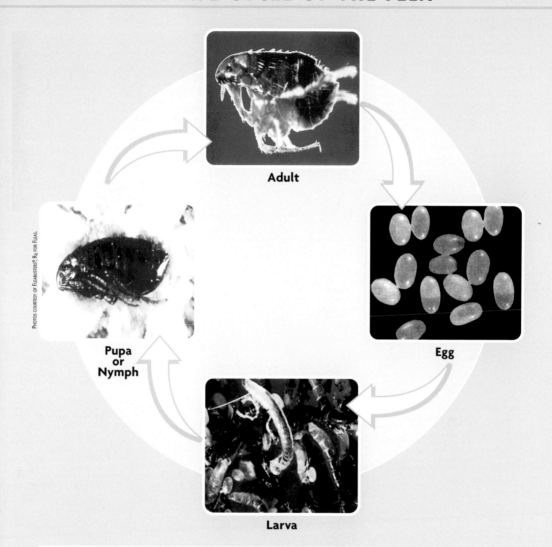

Adult

Egg

Larva

Pupa
or
Nymph

Photos courtesy of Fleabusters®, Rx for Fleas.

A LOOK AT FLEAS

Fleas have been around for millions of years and have adapted to
changing host animals. They are able to go through a complete life cycle
in less than one month or they can extend their lives to almost two years
by remaining as pupae or cocoons. They do not need blood or any other
food for up to 20 months.

INSECT GROWTH REGULATOR (IGR)

Two types of products should be used when treating fleas—a product to treat the pet and a product to treat the home. Adult fleas represent less than 1% of the flea population. The pre-adult fleas (eggs, larvae and pupae) represent more than 99% of the flea population and are found in the environment; it is in the case of pre-adult fleas that products containing an Insect Growth Regulator (IGR) should be used in the home.

IGRs are a new class of compounds used to prevent the development of insects. They do not kill the insect outright, but instead use the insect's biology against it to stop it from completing its growth. Products that contain methoprene are the world's first and leading IGRs. Used to control fleas and other insects, this type of IGR will stop flea larvae from developing and protect the house for up to seven months.

The American dog tick, *Dermacentor variabilis*, is probably the most common tick found on dogs. Look at the strength in its eight legs! No wonder it's hard to detach them.

adult insecticides are only active for a few days.

When treating with a house-hold spray, it is a good idea to vacuum before applying the product. This stimulates as many pupae as possible to hatch into adult fleas. The vacuum cleaner should also be treated with an insecticide to prevent the eggs and larvae that have been collected in the vacuum bag from hatching.

The second stage of treatment is to apply an adult insecticide to the dog. Traditionally, this would be in the form of a collar or a spray, but more recent innovations include digestible insecticides that poison the fleas when they ingest the dog's blood. Alternatively, there are drops that, when placed on the back of the dog's neck, spread throughout the dog's hair and skin to kill adult fleas.

TICKS

Though not as common as fleas, ticks are found all over the tropical and temperate world. They don't bite, like fleas; they harpoon. They dig their sharp proboscis (nose) into the dog's skin and drink the blood. Their

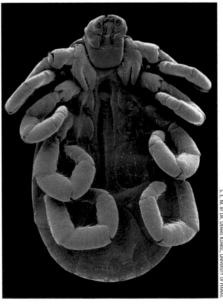

S. E. M. by Dr. Dennis Kunkel, University of Hawaii

only food and drink is dog's blood. Dogs can get Lyme disease, Rocky Mountain spotted fever, tick bite paralysis and many other diseases from ticks. They may live where fleas are found and they like to hide in cracks or seams in walls. They are controlled the same way fleas are controlled.

The American dog tick, *Dermacentor variabilis*, may well be the most common dog tick in many geographical areas, especially those areas where the climate is hot and humid. Most dog ticks have life expectancies of a week to six months, depending upon climatic conditions. They can neither jump nor fly, but they can crawl slowly and can range up to 16 feet to reach a sleeping or unsuspecting dog.

MITES

Just as fleas and ticks can be problematic for your dog, mites can also lead to an itchy nuisance. Microscopic in size, mites are related to ticks and generally take up permanent residence on their host animal—in this case, your dog! The term *mange* refers to any infestation caused by one of the mighty mites, of which there are six varieties that concern dog owners.

Demodex mites cause a condition known as demodicosis

DEER-TICK CROSSING
The great outdoors may be fun for your dog, but it also is home to dangerous ticks. Deer ticks carry a bacterium known as *Borrelia burgdorferi* and are most active in the autumn and spring. When infections are caught early, penicillin and tetracycline are effective antibiotics, but, if left untreated, the bacteria may cause neurological, kidney and cardiac problems as well as long-term trouble with walking and painful joints.

S. E. M. BY DR. ANDREW SPIELMAN/PHOTOTAKE.

PHOTO BY DR. DENNIS KUNKEL, UNIVERSITY OF HAWAII.

The head of an American dog tick, *Dermacentor variabilis*, enlarged and colorized for effect.

The mange mite, *Psoroptes bovis*, can infest cattle and other domestic animals.

PHOTO BY JAMES HAYDEN/YOAV/PHOTOTAKE

(sometimes called red mange or follicular mange), in which the mites live in the dog's hair follicles and sebaceous glands in larger-than-normal amounts. This type of mange is commonly passed from the dam to her puppies and usually shows up on the puppies' muzzles, though demodicosis is not transferable from one normal dog to another. Most dogs recover from this type of mange without any treatment, though topical therapies are commonly prescribed by the vet.

The *Cheyletiellosis* mite is the hook-mouthed culprit associated with "walking dandruff," a condition that affects dogs as well as cats and rabbits. This mite lives on the surface of the animal's skin and is readily transferable through direct or indirect contact with an affected animal. The dandruff is present in the form of scaly skin, which may or may not be itchy. If not treated, this mange can affect a whole kennel of dogs and can be spread to humans as well.

The *Sarcoptes* mite causes intense itching on the dog in the form of a condition known as scabies or sarcoptic mange. The cycle of the *Sarcoptes* mite lasts about three weeks, and the mites live in the top layer of the dog's skin (epidermis), preferably in

Human lice look like dog lice; the two are closely related.

PHOTO BY DWIGHT R. KUHN.

areas with little hair. Scabies is highly contagious and can be passed to humans. Sometimes an allergic reaction to the mite worsens the severe itching associated with sarcoptic mange.

Ear mites, *Otodectes cynotis,* lead to otodectic mange, which most commonly affects the outer ear canal of the dog, though other areas can be affected as well. Dogs with ear-mite infestation commonly scratch at their ears, causing further irritation, and shake their heads. Dark brown droppings in the outer ear confirm the diagnosis. Your vet can prescribe a treatment to flush out the ears and kill any eggs in the ears. A complete month of treatment is necessary to cure the mange.

Two other mites, less common in dogs, include *Dermanyssus gallinae* (the poultry or red mite) and *Eutrombicula alfreddugesi* (the North American mite associated with trombiculidiasis or chigger infestation). The poultry mite frequently lives on chickens, but can transfer to dogs who spend time near farm animals. Chigger infestation affects dogs in the

DO NOT MIX

Never mix parasite-control products without first consulting your vet. Some products can become toxic when combined with others and can cause fatal consequences.

NOT A DROP TO DRINK

Never allow your dog to swim in polluted water or public areas where water quality can be suspect. Even perfectly clear water can harbor parasites, many of which can cause serious to fatal illnesses in canines. Areas inhabited by water-fowl and other wildlife are especially dangerous.

central US who have exposure to woodlands. The types of mange caused by both of these mites are treatable by veterinarians.

INTERNAL PARASITES

Most animals—fishes, birds and mammals, including dogs and humans—have worms and other parasites that live inside their bodies. According to Dr. Herbert R. Axelrod, the fish pathologist, there are two kinds of parasites: dumb and smart. The smart parasites live in peaceful cooperation with their hosts (symbiosis), while the dumb parasites kill their hosts. Most worm infections are relatively easy to control. If they are not controlled, they weaken the host dog to the point that other medical problems occur, but they do not kill the host as dumb parasites would.

A brown dog tick, *Rhipicephalus sanguineus*, is an uncommon but annoying tick found on dogs.

PHOTO BY CAROLINA BIOLOGICAL SUPPLY/PHOTOTAKE.

PHOTO BY CAROLINA BIOLOGICAL SUPPLY/PHOTOTAKE.

The roundworm *Rhabditis* can infect both dogs and humans.

ROUNDWORMS

Average-size dogs can pass 1,360,000 roundworm eggs every day. For example, if there were only 1 million dogs in the world, the world would be saturated with thousands of tons of dog feces. These feces would contain around 15,000,000,000 roundworm eggs.

Up to 31% of home yards and children's sand boxes in the US contain roundworm eggs.

Flushing dog's feces down the toilet is not a safe practice because the usual sewage treatments do not destroy roundworm eggs.

Infected puppies start shedding roundworm eggs at three weeks of age. They can be infected by their mother's milk.

The roundworm, *Ascaris lumbricoides.*

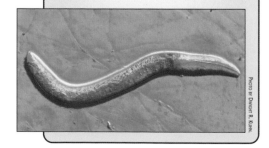

PHOTO BY DWIGHT R. KUHN.

ROUNDWORMS

The roundworms that infect dogs are known scientifically as *Toxocara canis*. They live in the dog's intestines and shed eggs continually. It has been estimated that a dog produces about 6 or more ounces of feces every day. Each ounce of feces averages hundreds of thousands of roundworm eggs. There are no known areas in which dogs roam that do not contain roundworm eggs. The greatest danger of roundworms is that they infect people, too! It is wise to have your dog tested regularly for roundworms.

In young puppies, roundworms cause bloated bellies, diarrhea, coughing and vomiting, and are transmitted from the dam (through blood or milk). Affected puppies will not appear as animated as normal puppies. The worms appear spaghetti-like, measuring as long as 6 inches. Adult dogs can acquire roundworms through coprophagia (eating contaminated feces) or by killing rodents that carry roundworms.

Roundworm infection can kill puppies and cause severe problems in adults, as the hatched larvae travel to the lungs and trachea through the bloodstream. Cleanliness is the best preventative for roundworms. Always pick up after your dog and dispose of feces in appropriate receptacles.

PHOTO BY DWIGHT R. KUHN.

HOOKWORMS

In the United States, dog owners have to be concerned about four different species of hookworm, the most common and most serious of which is *Ancylostoma caninum,* which prefers warm climates. The others are *Ancylostoma braziliense, Ancylostoma tubaeforme* and *Uncinaria stenocephala,* the latter of which is a concern to dogs living in the northern US and Canada, as this species prefers cold climates. Hookworms are dangerous to humans as well as to dogs and cats, and can be the cause of severe anemia due to iron deficiency. The worm uses its teeth to attach itself to the dog's intestines and changes the site of its attachment about six times per day. Each time the worm repositions itself, the dog loses

blood and can become anemic. *Ancylostoma caninum* is the most likely of the four species to cause anemia in the dog.

Symptoms of hookworm infection include dark stools, weight loss, general weakness, pale coloration and anemia, as well as possible skin problems. Fortunately, hookworms are easily purged from the affected dog with a number of medications that have proven effective. Discuss these with your veterinarian. Most heartworm preventatives include a hookworm insecticide as well.

Owners also must be aware that hookworms can infect humans, who can acquire the larvae through exposure to contaminated feces. Since the worms cannot complete their life cycle on a human, the worms simply infest the skin and cause irritation. This condition is known as cutaneous larva migrans syndrome. As a preventative, use disposable gloves or a "poop-scoop" to pick up your dog's droppings and prevent your dog (or neighborhood cats) from defecating in children's play areas.

The hookworm,, *Ancylostoma caninum.*

PHOTO BY C. JAMES WEBB/PHOTOTAKE.

The infective stage of the hookworm larva.

TAPEWORMS

Humans, rats, squirrels, foxes, coyotes, wolves and domestic dogs are all susceptible to tapeworm infection. Except in humans, tapeworms are usually not a fatal infection. Infected individuals can harbor 1000 parasitic worms.

Tapeworms, like some other types of worm, are hermaphroditic, meaning male and female in the same worm.

If dogs eat infected rats or mice, or anything else infected with tapeworm, they get the tapeworm disease. One month after attaching to a dog's intestine, the worm starts shedding eggs. These eggs are infective immediately. Infective eggs can live for a few months without a host animal.

The head and rostellum (the round prominence on the scolex) of a tapeworm, which infects dogs and humans.

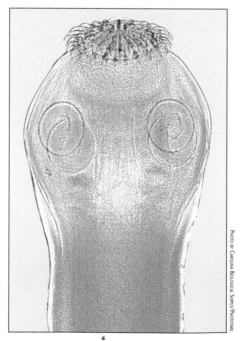

PHOTO BY CAROLINA BIOLOGICAL SUPPLY/PHOTOTAKE

TAPEWORMS

There are many species of tapeworm, all of which are carried by fleas! The most common tapeworm affecting dogs is known as *Dipylidium caninum*. The dog eats the flea and starts the tapeworm cycle. Humans can also be infected with tapeworms—so don't eat fleas! Fleas are so small that your dog could pass them onto your hands, your plate or your food and thus make it possible for you to ingest a flea that is carrying tapeworm eggs.

While tapeworm infection is not life-threatening in dogs (smart parasite!), it can be the cause of a very serious liver disease for humans. About 50% of the humans infected with *Echinococcus multilocularis*, a type of tapeworm that causes alveolar hydatid, perish.

WHIPWORMS

In North America, whipworms are counted among the most common parasitic worms in dogs. The whipworm's scientific name is *Trichuris vulpis*. These worms attach themselves in the lower parts of the intestine, where they feed. Affected dogs may only experience upset tummies, colic and diarrhea. These worms, however, can live for months or years in the dog, beginning their larval stage in the small intestine, spending their adult stage in the large intestine and finally passing infective eggs through the dog's feces. The only way to detect whipworms is through a fecal examination, though this is not always foolproof. Treatment for whipworms is tricky, due to the worms' unusual life-cycle pattern, and very often dogs are reinfected due to exposure to infective eggs on the ground. The whipworm eggs can survive in the environment for as long as five years; thus, cleaning up droppings in your own backyard as well as in public places is absolutely essential for sanitation purposes and the health of your dog and others.

THREADWORMS
Though less common than roundworms, hookworms and those previously mentioned, threadworms concern dog owners in the southwestern US and Gulf Coast area, where the climate is hot and humid. Living in the small intestine of the dog, this worm measures a mere 2 millimeters and is round in shape. Like that of the whipworm, the threadworm's life cycle is very complex and the eggs and larvae are passed through the feces. A deadly disease in humans, *Strongyloides* readily infects people, and the handling of feces is the most common means of transmission. Threadworms are most often seen in young puppies; bloody diarrhea and pneumonia are symptoms. Sick puppies must be isolated and treated immediately; vets recommend a follow-up treatment one month later.

HEARTWORM PREVENTATIVES

There are many heartworm preventatives on the market, many of which are sold at your veterinarian's office. These products can be given daily or monthly, depending on the manufacturer's instructions. All of these preventatives contain chemical insecticides directed at killing heartworms, which leads to some controversy among dog owners. In effect, heartworm preventatives are necessary evils, though you should determine how necessary based on your pet's lifestyle. There is no doubt that heartworm is a dreadful disease that threatens the lives of dogs. However, the likelihood of your dog's being bitten by an infected mosquito is slim in most places, and a mosquito-repellent (or an herbal remedy such as Wormwood or Black Walnut) is much safer for your dog and will not compromise his immune system (the way heartworm preventatives will). Should you decide to use the traditional preventative "medications," you can consider giving the pill every other or third month. Since the toxins in the pill will kill the heartworms at all stages of development, the pill would be effective in killing larvae, nymphs or adults and it takes four months for the larvae to reach the adult stage. Thus, there is no rationale to poisoning the dog's system on a monthly basis. Lastly, do not give the pill during the winter months since there are no mosquitoes around to pass on their infection, unless you live in a tropical environment.

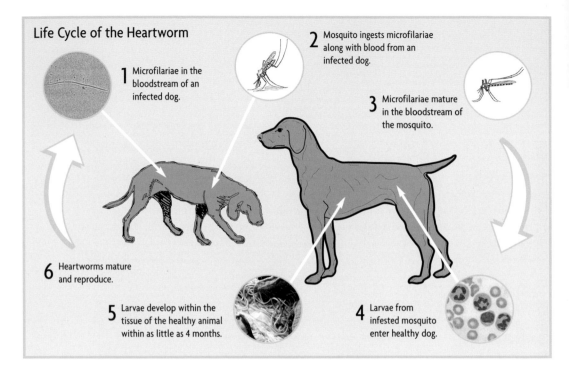

Life Cycle of the Heartworm

1 Microfilariae in the bloodstream of an infected dog.

2 Mosquito ingests microfilariae along with blood from an infected dog.

3 Microfilariae mature in the bloodstream of the mosquito.

4 Larvae from infested mosquito enter healthy dog.

5 Larvae develop within the tissue of the healthy animal within as little as 4 months.

6 Heartworms mature and reproduce.

HEARTWORMS

Heartworms are thin, extended worms up to 12 inches long, which live in a dog's heart and the major blood vessels surrounding it. Dogs may have up to 200 worms. Symptoms may be loss of energy, loss of appetite, coughing, the development of a pot belly and anemia.

Heartworms are transmitted by mosquitoes. The mosquito drinks the blood of an infected dog and takes in larvae with the blood. The larvae, called microfilariae, develop within the body of the mosquito and are passed on to the next dog bitten after the larvae mature. It takes two to three weeks for the larvae to develop to the infective stage within the body of the mosquito. Dogs are usually treated at about six weeks of age and maintained on a prophylactic dose given monthly.

Blood testing for heartworms is not necessarily indicative of how seriously your dog is infected. Although this is a dangerous disease, it is not easy for a dog to be infected. Discuss the various preventatives with your vet, as there are many different types now available. Together you can decide on a safe course of prevention for your dog.

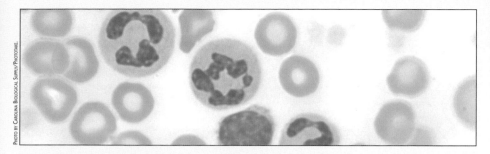

Magnified heartworm larvae, *Dirofilaria immitis.*

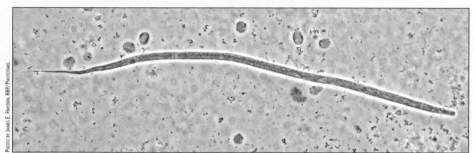

Heartworm, *Dirofilaria immitis.*

The heart of a dog infected with canine heartworm, *Dirofilaria immitis.*

HOMEOPATHY:
an alternative
to conventional
medicine

"Less is Most"

Using this principle, the strength of a homeopathic remedy is measured by the number of serial dilutions that were undertaken to create it. The greater the number of serial dilutions, the greater the strength of the homeopathic remedy. The potency of a remedy that has been made by making a dilution of 1 part in 100 parts (or 1/100) is 1c or 1cH. If this remedy is subjected to a series of further dilutions, each one being 1/100, a more dilute and stronger remedy is produced. If the remedy is diluted in this way six times, it is called 6c or 6cH. A dilution of 6c is 1 part in 1,000,000,000,000. In general, higher potencies in more frequent doses are better for acute symptoms and lower potencies in more infrequent doses are more useful for chronic, long-standing problems.

CURING OUR DOGS NATURALLY

Holistic medicine means treating the whole animal as a unique, perfect, living being. Generally, holistic treatments do not suppress the symptoms that the body naturally produces, as do most medications prescribed by conventional doctors and vets. Holistic methods seek to cure disease by regaining balance and harmony in the patient's environment. Some of these methods include use of nutritional therapy, herbs, flower essences, aromatherapy, acupuncture, massage, chiropractic and, of course, the most popular holistic approach, homeopathy.

Homeopathy is a theory or system of treating illness with small doses of substances which, if administered in larger quantities, would produce the symptoms that the patient already has. This approach is often described as "like cures like." Although modern veterinary medicine is geared toward the "quick fix," homeopathy relies on the belief that, given the time, the body is able to heal itself and return to its natural, healthy state.

Choosing a remedy to cure a problem in our dogs is the difficult part of homeopathy. Consult with your vet for a professional diagnosis of your dog's symptoms. Often these symptoms require immediate conventional care. If your vet is willing and knowledgeable, you may attempt a homeopathic remedy. Be aware that cortisone prevents homeopathic remedies from working. There are hundreds of possibilities and combinations to cure many problems in dogs, from basic physical problems such as excessive shedding, fleas or other parasites, unattractive doggy odor, bad breath, upset tummy, obesity, dry, oily or dull coat, diarrhea, ear problems or eye discharge (including tears and dry or mucousy matter), to behavioral abnormalities such as fear of loud noises, habitual licking, poor appetite, excessive barking and various phobias. From alumina to zincum metallicum, the remedies span the planet and the imagination…from flowers and weeds to chemicals, insect droppings, diesel smoke and volcanic ash.

Using "Like to Treat Like"

Unlike conventional medicines that suppress symptoms, homeopathic remedies treat illnesses with small doses of substances that, if administered in larger quantities, would produce the symptoms that the patient already has. While the same homeopathic remedy can be used to treat different symptoms in different dogs, here are some interesting remedies and their uses.

Apis Mellifica
(made from honey bee venom) can be used for allergies or to reduce swelling that occurs in acutely infected kidneys.

Diesel Smoke
can be used to help control travel sickness.

Calcarea Fluorica
(made from calcium fluoride, which helps harden bone structure) can be useful in treating hard lumps in tissues.

Natrum Muriaticum
(made from common salt, sodium chloride) is useful in treating thin, thirsty dogs.

Nitricum Acidum
(made from nitric acid) is used for symptoms you would expect to see from contact with acids, such as lesions, especially where the skin joins the linings of body orifices or openings such as the lips and nostrils.

Symphytum
(made from the herb Knitbone, *Symphytum officianale*) is used to encourage bones to heal.

Urtica Urens
(made from the common stinging nettle) is used in treating painful, irritating rashes.

MASTIFF

The first concept that the canine novice learns when watching a dog show is that each dog first competes against members of his own breed. Once the judge has selected the best member of each breed (Best of Breed), provided that the show is judged on a Group system, that chosen dog will compete with other dogs in his group. Finally, the dogs chosen first in each group will compete for Best in Show.

The second concept that you must understand is that the dogs are not actually compared against one another. The judge compares each dog against his breed standard, the written description of the ideal specimen that is approved by the American Kennel Club (AKC). While some early breed standards were indeed based on specific dogs that were famous or popular, many dedicated enthusiasts say that a perfect specimen, as described in the standard, has never walked into a show ring, has never been bred and, to the woe of dog breeders around the globe, does not exist. Breeders attempt to get as close to this ideal as possible with every litter, but theoretically the "perfect" dog is so elusive that it is impossible.

If you are interested in exploring the world of dog showing, your best bet is to join your local breed club or the national parent club, which is the Mastiff Club of America. These clubs often host both regional and national specialties, shows only for Mastiffs, which can include conformation as well as obedience and other performance events. Even if you have no intention of competing with your Mastiff, a specialty is a like a festival for lovers of the breed who congregate to share their favorite topic: the Mastiff! Clubs also send out newsletters, and some organize training days and seminars in order that people may learn more about their chosen breed. To locate the breed club closest to you, contact the American Kennel Club, which furnishes the rules and regulations for all of these events plus general dog registration and other basic requirements of dog ownership.

In the US, the American Kennel Club offers three kinds of

The dog that the judge deems to be closest to the breed standard wins his class. This dog continues on for Best of Breed and, in a Group show, then competes for Best in Group and finally Best in Show.

conformation shows: an all-breed show (for all AKC-recognized breeds), a specialty show (for one breed only, usually sponsored by the parent club) and a Group show (for all breeds in the group; this is the Working Group for the Mastiff). For a dog to become an AKC champion of record, the dog must accumulate 15 points at the shows from at least three different judges, including two "majors." A "major" is defined as a three-, four- or five-point win, and the number of points per win is determined by the number of dogs entered in the show on that day. Depending on the breed, the number of points that are awarded varies. More dogs are needed to rack up the points in more popular breeds, and less dogs are needed in less popular breeds.

At any dog show, only one dog and one bitch of each breed can win points. Dog showing does not offer "co-ed" classes. Dogs and bitches never compete against each other in the classes. Non-champion dogs are called "class dogs" because they compete in one of five classes. Dogs are entered in a particular class depending on age and previous show wins. To begin, there is the Puppy Class (for 6- to 9-month-olds and for 9- to 12-month-olds); this class is followed by the Novice Class (for dogs that have not won any first prizes except in the Puppy Class or three first

CLUB CONTACTS

You can get information about dog shows from the national kennel clubs:

American Kennel Club
5580 Centerview Dr., Raleigh, NC 27606-3390
www.akc.org

United Kennel Club
100 E. Kilgore Road, Kalamazoo, MI 49002
www.ukcdogs.com

Canadian Kennel Club
89 Skyway Ave., Suite 100, Etobicoke, Ontario M9W 6R4 Canada
www.ckc.ca

Fédération Cynologique Internationale
14, rue Leopold II, B-6530 Thuin, Belgium
www.fci.be

prizes in the Novice Class and have not accumulated any points toward their champion title); the Bred-by Exhibitor Class (for dogs handled by their breeders or by one of the breeder's immediate family); the American-bred Class (for dogs bred in the US); and the Open Class (for any dog that is not a champion).

The judge at the show begins judging the Puppy Class, first dogs and then bitches, and proceeds through the classes. The judge places his winners first through fourth in each class. In the Winners Class, the first-place winners of each class compete with one another to determine Winners Dog and Winners Bitch.

The judge also places a Reserve Winners Dog and Reserve Winners Bitch, which could be awarded the points in the case of a disqualification. The Winners Dog and Winners Bitch are the two that are awarded the points for the breed, then compete with any champions of record (often called "specials") entered in the show. The judge reviews the Winners Dog, Winners Bitch and all of the champions to select his Best of Breed. The Best of Winners is selected between the Winners Dog and Winners Bitch. Were one of these two to be selected Best of Breed, he or she would automatically be named Best of Winners as well. Finally the judge selects his Best of Opposite Sex to the Best of Breed winner.

At a Group show or all-breed show, the Best of Breed winners from each breed then compete against one another for Group One through Group Four. The judge compares each Best of Breed to its breed standard, and the dog that most closely lives up to the ideal for his breed is selected as Group

The Mastiff is a massive and proportionately consructed dog, with an impressive head and an overall air of dignity. These are the traits of a champion.

One. Finally, all seven group winners (from the Working Group, Toy Group, Hound Group, etc.) compete for Best in Show.

To find out about dog shows in your area, you can subscribe to the American Kennel Club's monthly magazine, the *American Kennel Gazette,* and the accompanying Events Calendar. You can also look in your local newspaper for advertisements for dog shows in your area or go on the Internet to the AKC's website, www.akc.org.

If your Mastiff is six months of age or older and registered with the AKC, you can enter him a dog show where the breed is offered classes. Provided that your Mastiff does not have a disqualifying fault, he can compete. Only unal-

AKC GROUPS

For showing purposes, the American Kennel Club divides his recognized breeds into seven groups: Working Dogs, Sporting Dogs, Hounds, Terriers, Toys, Non-Sporting Dogs and Herding Dogs.

SHOW-RING ETIQUETTE

Just as with anything else, there is a certain etiquette to the show ring that can only be learned through experience. Showing your dog can be quite intimidating to you as a novice when it seems as if everyone else knows what he is doing. You can familiarize yourself with ring procedure beforehand by taking showing classes to prepare you and your dog for conformation showing and by talking with experienced handlers. When you are in the ring, it is very important to pay attention and listen to the instructions you are given by the judge about where to move your dog. Remember, even the most skilled handlers had to start somewhere. Keep it up and you too will become a proficient handler as you gain practice and experience.

tered dogs can be entered in a dog show, so if you have spayed or neutered your Mastiff, you cannot compete in conformation shows. The reason for this is simple. Dog shows are the main forum to prove which representatives of a breed are worthy of being bred. Only dogs that have achieved championships—the AKC "seal of approval" for quality in pure-bred dogs—should be bred. Altered dogs, however, can participate in other AKC events such as obedience trials and the Canine Good Citizen program.

Before you actually step into the ring, you would be well advised to sit back and observe the judge's ring procedure. If it is your first time in the ring, do not be over-anxious and run to the front of the line. It is much better to stand back and study how the exhibitor in front of you is performing. The judge asks each handler to "stack" the dog, hopefully showing the dog off to his best advantage. The judge will observe the dog from a distance and from different angles, and approach the dog to check his teeth, overall structure, alertness and muscle tone, as well as consider how well the dog "conforms" to the standard. Most importantly, the judge will have the exhibitor move the dog around the ring in some pattern that he should specify (another advantage to not going first, but always listen since some judges change their directions—and the judge is always right!). Finally, the judge will give the dog one last look before moving on to the next exhibitor.

If you are not in the top four in your class at your first show, do not be discouraged. Be patient and consistent, and you may eventually find yourself in a winning line-up. Remember that the winners were once in your shoes and have devoted many hours and much money to earn the placement. If you find that your dog is losing every time and never getting a nod, it may be time to consider a different dog

sport or to just enjoy your Mastiff as a pet. Parent clubs offer other events, such as agility, obedience, instinct tests and more, which may be of interest to the owner of a well-trained Mastiff.

BEYOND CONFORMATION

OBEDIENCE TRIALS
Obedience trials in the US trace back to the early 1930s when organized obedience training was developed to demonstrate how well dog and owner could work together. The pioneer of obedience trials is Mrs. Helen Whitehouse Walker, a Standard Poodle fancier, who designed a series of exercises

To determine the physical soundness of a show dog, the judge assesses the dog's movement while the handler gaits the dog around the ring.

after the Associated Sheep, Police Army Dog Society of Great Britain. Since the days of Mrs. Walker, obedience trials have grown by leaps and bounds, and today there are over 2,000 trials held in the US every year, with more than 100,000 dogs competing. Any registered AKC dog can enter an obedience trial, regardless of conformational disqualifications or neutering.

Obedience trials are divided into three levels of progressive difficulty. At the first level, the Novice, dogs compete for the title Companion Dog (CD); at the intermediate level, the Open, dogs compete for the title Companion Dog Excellent (CDX); and at the advanced level, the Utility, dogs compete for the title Utility Dog (UD). Classes are sub-divided into "A" (for beginners) and "B" (for more experienced handlers). A perfect score at any level is 200, and a dog must score 170 or better to earn a "leg," of which three are needed to earn the title. To earn points, the dog must score more than 50% of the available points in each exercise; the possible points range from 20 to 40.

Once a dog has earned the UD title, he can compete with other proven obedience dogs for the coveted title of Utility Dog Excellent (UDX), which requires that the dog win "legs" in ten shows. Utility Dogs who earn "legs" in Open B and Utility B earn points toward their Obedience Trial Champion title. In 1977, the title Obedience Trial Champion (OTCh.) was established by the AKC. To become an OTCh., a dog needs to earn 100 points, which requires three first places in Open B and Utility under three different judges.

The Grand Prix of obedience trials, the AKC National Obedience Invitational gives qualifying Utility Dogs the chance to win the newest and highest title: National Obedience Champion (NOC). Only the top 25 ranked obedience dogs, plus any dog ranked in the top 3 in his breed, are allowed to compete.

AGILITY TRIALS

Having had its origins in the UK back in 1977, AKC agility had its official beginning in the US in August 1994, when the first licensed agility trials were held. The AKC allows all registered breeds (including Miscellaneous Class breeds) to participate, providing the dog is 12 months of age or older. Agility is designed so that the handler demonstrates how well the dog can work at his side. The handler directs his dog over an obstacle course that includes jumps as well as tires, the dog walk, weave poles, pipe tunnels, collapsed tunnels, etc. While working his way through the course, the dog must keep one eye and ear on the handler and the rest of his body on the course. The handler gives verbal and hand signals to guide the dog through the course.

The first organization to promote agility trials in the US was the United States Dog Agility Association, Inc. (USDAA), which was established in 1986 and spawned numerous member clubs around the country. Both the USDAA and the American Kennel Club offer titles to winning dogs.

Agility is great fun for dog and owner, with many rewards for everyone involved. If you are interested, once your Mastiff has reached the appropriate age to begin agility training, you should join a training club that has obstacles and experienced agility handlers who can introduce you and your dog to the "ropes" (and tires, tunnels, etc.).

TRACKING

Any dog is capable of tracking, using his nose to follow a trail. Tracking tests are exciting and competitive ways to test your Mastiff's instinctive scenting ability and his ability to search and rescue. The AKC started tracking tests in 1937, when the first AKC-licensed test took place as part of the Utility level at an obedience trial. Ten years later in 1947, the AKC offered the first title, Tracking Dog (TD). It was not until 1980 that the AKC added the title Tracking Dog Excellent

(TDX), which was followed by the title Versatile Surface Tracking (VST) in 1995. The title Champion Tracker (CT) is awarded to a dog who has earned all three titles.

In the beginning level of tracking, the owner follows the dog through a field on a long lead. To earn the TD title, the dog must follow a track laid by a human 30 to 120 minutes prior. The track is about 500 yards with up to 5 directional changes. The TDX requires that the dog follow a track that is 3 to 5 hours old over a course up to 1,000 yards with up to 7 directional changes. The VST requires that the dog follow a track up to 5 hours old through an urban setting.

Practicing at home with your Mastiff will help both of you develop the needed skills and confidence for the show ring.

WORKING TITLES

The Mastiff Club of America (MCOA) developed a program through which Mastiffs can earn titles of Working Dog, Working Dog Excellent and Working Dog Supreme. Although the AKC does not offer working titles, the MCOA's aim is to show the world that the Mastiff is still truly a working breed by encouraging versatility and awarding titles to dogs who have proven, through achievement in different areas, that they possess all of the attributes of a capable and noble working animal. Among these traits are correct conformation, sound temperament, trainablility and participation in different venues, e.g., obedience, tracking, agility, therapy work, Canine Good Citizen certifcation, etc.

In order to earn one of the three titles, a dog must earn points (100 for WD; 200 for WDX; 300 for WDSupreme) according to a point schedule set forth by the MCOA. The points must come from achievement in each of four different categories: Obedience, Temperament, Tracking/Agility and Specialty. Achievement in the Obedience and Tracking/Agility categories is determined by titles earned in competition held by the American Kennel Club, United Kennel Club and/or Continental Kennel Club, with higher level titles' holding higher point values. The Temperament category requires the dog to have passed an approved temperament test or to have earned AKC Canine Good Citizen certification. The Specialty category offers a variety of ways for a dog to earn points, including conformation championships and participation in programs such as search and rescue and therapy work.

In order for owners to apply for working titles on their Mastiffs, they must submit to the MCOA a completed application and copies of the dogs' certifications in the required areas (temperament certification, title certificates, etc.).

FÉDÉRATION CYNOLOGIQUE INTERNATIONALE

Established in 1911, the Fédération Cynologique Internationale (FCI) represents the "world kennel club." This international body brings uniformity to the breeding, judging and showing of pure-bred dogs. Although the FCI originally included only five European nations: France, Germany, Austria, the Netherlands and Belgium (which remains its headquarters), the organization today embraces nations on six continents and recognizes well over 300 breeds of pure-bred dog.

The FCI sponsors both national and international shows. The hosting country determines the judging system and breed standards are always based on the breed's country of origin. Dogs from every country can participate in these impressive canine spectacles, the largest of which is the World Dog Show, hosted in a different country each year.

There are three titles attainable through the FCI: the International Champion, which is the most prestigious; the International Beauty Champion, which is based on aptitude certificates in different countries; and the International Trial Champion, which is based on achievement in obedience trials in different countries. An FCI title requires a dog to win three CACs (*Certificats d'Aptitude au Championnat*), at regional or club shows under three different judges who are breed specialists. The title of International Champion is gained by winning four CACIBs (*Certificats d'Aptitude au Championnat International de Beauté*) which are offered only at international shows, with at least a one-year lapse between the first and fourth award.

The FCI is divided into ten groups and the Mastiff is shown in Group 2 with the Molossians. At the World Dog Show, the following classes are offered for each breed: Puppy Class (6–9 months), Junior Class (9–18 months), Open Class (15 months or older) and Champion Class. A dog can be awarded a classifica-

Aside from the excitement of the ring, participating in dog shows affords you the opportunity to meet and share your love of the breed with other Mastiff fanciers.

tion of Excellent, Very Good, Good, Sufficient and Not Sufficient. Puppies can be awarded classifications of Very Promising, Promising or Not Promising. Four placements are made in each class. After all classes are judged, a Best of Breed is selected. Other special groups and classes may also be shown. Each exhibitor showing a dog receives a written evaluation from the judge.

Besides the World Dog Show and other all-breed shows, you can exhibit your dog at specialty shows held by different breed clubs. Specialty shows may have their own regulations.

INDEX

My Mastiff

PUT YOUR PUPPY'S FIRST PICTURE HERE

Dog's Name _____

Date _____ Photographer _____